Unitarian Universalism:

A Narrative History

by David E. Bumbaugh

 Meadville Lombard Press - Chicago

ISBN: 0-9702479-0-7

book cover design by Micah T.J. Jackson
book layout by Elissa Leone
fonts used in this publication: Book Antiqua, 11

DEDICATION

This work is dedicated to the memory of Dr. Donald K. Evans, who introduced me to Universalism, and to Dr. John C. Godbey, who awakened in me a love of Unitarian History.

ACKNOWLEDGEMENTS

I wish to thank the congregation of the Unitarian Church in Summit, New Jersey (Unitarian Universalist) for granting the sabbatical which made it possible to begin this work; to Meadville Lombard Theological School for making possible its publication; and to the St. Lawrence Foundation for Theological Education for its supporting grant. I am grateful to the many colleagues and parishioners who have encouraged me over the years to undertake this project. My special thanks go to Elissa Leone, Kathryn Bert, Anthony David and Micah Jackson for their technical assistance, and to my wife Beverly, who, with great patience, has lived with this project and read and reread the various versions making invaluable suggestions along the way.

DEB

TABLE OF CONTENTS

FOREWORD

Both students and general readers will find this history by David Bumbaugh a welcome addition to the historiography of liberal religion. His kaleidoscopic coverage of religious developments in Europe in the period of the Protestant Reformation clarifies for the reader the forces that led Michael Servetus, Francis David, among many others, to insist that the purification of the Christian church would not be complete until it rid itself of doctrines, such as that of the Trinity, that had no biblical basis. For this audacity, several paid with their lives.

The porous borders of the day allowed for easy movement by those who sought to challenge church practices long accepted by the populace. It is striking that one of the most influential dissents came from the Italian city-states, so often dominated by the papacy. If I may be allowed a personal note in this regard: In reading Professor Bumbaugh's manuscript, I was reminded that, in the days before the merger of the Universalist Church of America and the American Unitarian Association, I had the occasion to spend several days in hospital for the treatment of a malady the nature of which memory, with its marvelous ways, refuses me recall. During that stay, I was questioned by a nurse as to why a person with a name such as mine would list himself on the hospital's forms as a "Unitarian," when she would have expected to read "Roman Catholic." Since her surname struck me as Italianate, I had the mischievous pleasure of pointing out to her that the European Unitarian movement was christened with the name of two Italians, uncle and nephew, Fausto and Lelio Sozzini, or, as the Latin form had it, Socinus. Her incredulous eyes were shocked that evening, when, checking the family encyclopedia, she learned that I had not been joking.

Unitarianism, in Socinian or other forms, took hold in diverse places across the continent, Poland, Transylvania, the Netherlands, particularly becoming hotbeds of the faith, challenging the old ways of thinking.

Socinianism then found its way across the channel to Britain, and, in the early nineteenth century, the orthodox in the New England Congregational churches were to tar their liberal brethren with its brush, although the latter indignantly resisted the label.

As Professor Bumbaugh recounts it, the story of the spread of Socinianism across Europe makes fascinating reading, as does his coverage of the rise and development of liberal religion in the American colonies and the United States. It is at this point that Universalism comes into the picture. It had its advocates in the early centuries of Christianity, and could be found here and there in Europe among thinkers who rejected the dour teaching of Calvinism that the greater number of humanity were destined for the fiery depths of an eternal hell. These brave souls went against the grain of orthodoxy by insisting that God was a beneficent being who would save all of His children. Although John Murray, who migrated from England in 1770, is looked back on fondly as the father of Universalism in America, the story is much more complicated. There were several outcroppings of belief in the salvation of all souls independent of the Englishman's efforts, but it was his vigorous advocacy in travels up and down the east coast, even after he made his home in Gloucester, and then in Boston, that was largely responsible for its notoriety, and the establishment of the churches that would develop into a new denomination.

The second generation Universalist Hosea Ballou, under the influence of the Enlightenment and Deism, was to bring into the movement insistence on the use of reason in the interpretation of biblical texts, and the resultant rejection of the doctrine of the Trinity. Ballou propagated unitarian views among the Universalists at the same time that theological commotions among the Congregationalists were to result in the gradual separation of the orthodox and Unitarian churches. One of the more fascinating aspects of this story is that the two most prominent advocates of the respective approaches to liberal religion, Unitarian William Ellery Channing and Universalist Hosea Ballou, were ensconced in Boston in the first half of the nineteenth century and locked horns, in the press, but not in person, in the formative years of the two movements.

As one of Professor Bumbaugh's distinguished predecessors on the faculty of the Meadville Lombard Theological School, Charles H. Lyttle, was to put it, "Freedom Moves West." Jefferson's Louisiana Purchase doubled the size of the original United States, and the seizure of the greater part of Mexico by American forces under President Polk, presented a challenge to the two liberal religious movements, as they attempted to bring their respective gospels to the population as it settled across a vast landscape. Then, of course, there was the agony of the Civil War, which created bitter divisions in churches North and South.

Universalists and Unitarians are so fond of their early history, they often neglect later developments. One of the big advantages of this history is that Professor Bumbaugh brings the history down to the present day. He explains the tensions between some Unitarians and Universalists before the merger of the denominations in 1961, the latter fearing they would be swallowed up by the stronger partner. After merger, the contest for the hearts and minds of liberals between theists and humanists continued over into the new denomination. In recent times, a humanistically-inclined denomination has found developing within it new interpretations of liberal religion, among them a vague emotion labeled "spirituality," and an earth-centered approach to religion, labeled "pagan." Of course, as one would expect, there is a continuing concern over the relation of the denomination to its Christian roots.

It is not the purpose of a Foreword to recapitulate the entire thrust of the work in hand. Readers will do that for themselves. The readers of this book will find the history of the two liberal movements, and then of the united movement, retold in a concise, intelligent, manner, with David Bumbaugh's keen insights and graceful prose.

Ernest Cassara
Professor Emeritus of History
& former Chair of the Department of History
George Mason University

UNITARIAN UNIVERSALISM

Unitarian Universalism is a peculiar religious tradition in that what binds it is not so much a shared theology, or even a shared response to the experience of the sacred, as it is a shared history. We are one people because of our inchoate understanding of the journey through time which we share. This is not to suggest that we are always accurate about the history we claim, or that we always understand the motives, the behaviors, the attitudes of those who have preceded us, but rather that we are enraptured by a mythic sense of having shared a journey which began by rejecting conventional views and has been defined by a continuing struggle toward a personally satisfying understanding of the self, of the nature of the human venture, of the meaning of existence.

Thus, most of our heroes speak a tongue we do not fully understand, but they represent for us a validation of our own experience. Few of us know much of the theology of Servetus, Socinus, David, or Biandrata, and would reject much of those theologies if we did understand them. But we know that our ancestors in the period of the Reformation were heroic souls who went out from the safety of the Roman church, who tarried only a while in the confines of more conventional Protestantism, and who dared to carve out a religious response to the times which reflected their own individual experience. It is this we have in common with them, and it is this sense of historical continuity which makes of us a movement. (It is also this which tempts us to adopt people who were never part of our movement but whose personal histories make us think they might have been Unitarian Universalists, or would have been if they had had the opportunity.)

Because we are defined by a common story rather than a common theology, and because that story has shaped our institutions in significant ways, we offer here an extended survey of Unitarian Universalist history. This is not intended to be a scholarly exposition, but rather a restatement of the myth at the heart of our movement. It will not replace the need to read scholarly histories, but it seeks to provide the common background from which an exploration of the polity, practices and convictions of contemporary Unitarian Universalists may be understood and examined.

Unitarian Universalism in Europe[1]

The Beginnings

Those who seek the roots of Unitarian Universalism must begin in the early years of the Christian church. Some enthusiasts have sought to discover proto-Unitarians in the court of Pharaoh Akhenaten and proto-Universalists among the pre-Socratic Greek philosophers. Undoubtedly, this effort demands more imagination than scholarship. There can be no doubt, however, that the theological conflicts which gave shape to early Unitarianism and Universalism can be seen as reflections of controversies which afflicted the very early church. At the risk of extreme over-simplification, let us sketch the circumstances and issues that were to prove central to Unitarianism and Universalism.

The central concept to remember is that Christianity, however we understand its evolution, did not come into being with a full-blown organizational structure or theological system intact. Early Christianity seems to have emerged from pre-rabbinic Judaism in various urban centers of the Roman Empire. It may also have roots in the burial societies and associations which were common among the lower classes of urban society, and which often centered upon patrons in whose homes the societies met. Whatever the root of nascent Christianity, there was no central authority, no commonly accepted scripture, no commonly practiced liturgy, and no orthodox theology. Indeed, earliest Christianity encompassed a diversity of opinion, practice and belief—a diversity that would return to haunt the church after Christianity became established.

It would appear that among the issues which divided various communities of Christians, were both organizational practices and fundamental theological convictions. The texts from the New Testament and the writings of the early church reflect a variety of organizational styles and patterns. The controversies that afflicted the early years of the church demonstrate beyond doubt that there was no single standard of belief among early Christians. Among the issues which vexed the early Christian communities were those which centered upon the nature of Jesus of Nazareth. Was he the latest in a long line of prophets calling the human community to righteousness and piety or was he something more? If he were only a prophet, then how justify a separate community? If he were more than just another prophet, how was that something more to be understood and defined. In short, what was the nature of Jesus, called the Christ and how was he to be related to God.

Without attempting to describe the many competing answers to these questions that arose among the various Christian communities, let me suggest that there seemed to be an early consensus that Jesus could not be understood as simply human. However, the nature of his unique quality, the definition of his relationship to God, the problem of relating a more-than-human Jesus to a monotheistic God seemed to defy consensus. When the issue came to a head at the Council of Nicaea (325 c.e.), this first ecumenical council was faced with two major positions—that of Arius, who affirmed that Jesus was more than human, but denied that he was equal to or co-existent with God; and that of Athanasius who insisted that Jesus was co-equal with God.

The Arians lost the struggle for the soul and mind of the church, but the major effect of their persistent struggle was to shift the center of Christianity from an ethical to a creedal religion, concerned less with character than with correctness of belief. The Council of Nicaea began the process which would eventuate in the Doctrine of the Trinity, the teaching that Jesus was fully god and fully man, that god, while one in nature was manifested as God the Father, God the Son (Jesus Christ), and God the Holy Spirit, of one substance, co-eternal. Just as the rites and observances of the early church drew heavily upon Hellenistic mystery religions, and the organizational patterns of the early church evolved out of voluntary associations within the urban centers of the Roman Empire[2], so this central theological formulation was rooted in Greek philosophy and Hellenistic thought.

Those who were unwilling to accept the Doctrine of the Trinity did not give up quietly. The struggle went on with the Arians dominating the Eastern Empire for decades. But in the end, they were banished to the fringes of the empire, where, particularly in the Balkans, they carried their peculiar understanding of Christianity to the indigenous peoples of the area. In some defining ways, the Arians were the "god-parents" of Unitarianism, and when Unitarianism emerged from the maelstrom of the Protestant Reformation, that religious formulation was often called "Arianism" by its opponents

The other strand of our tradition, Universalism, is also rooted in the divergent opinions of the early church. Whoever Jesus may have been, an essential question concerns the purpose of his appearance on earth. There is some reason to believe that significant portions of the early church embraced the view that the Christ came to call all people to renewed harmony with the God from whom they had been so profoundly alienated. Some hint of that conviction can be found in the New Testament itself—in the assertion that "It is not God's will that any should perish, but that *all* should be made the sons of God," in the promise that "as in Adam all died, so in Christ shall *all* be made to live again," and in the conviction that before Jesus "*every* knee shall bow and *every* tongue confess." [3]

Beyond this, the writings of the early church fathers—especially Clement and Origen of Alexandria—expressed the conviction that in the fullness of time all of creation would be restored to harmony with God[4]. This Universalism, the doctrine of the ultimate salvation of all, presents a compelling mystic vision, but it is a weak foundation upon which to construct a militant, disciplined, missionary-minded religious movement. If, in the end, all are to be restored to harmony with God, it becomes less urgent that all on earth accept the same doctrines, practice the same liturgy, obey the same priestly decrees. In the end, Universalism would be damned as heresy, and even Origen would be denounced as a heretic.[5]

These are the convictions that gave rise to the two strands which, over time, would result in Unitarianism and Universalism as distinct theological and religious options. Although both were considered heretical as the ancient world gave way to the medieval, neither conviction ever disappeared from the thinking of Christianity. Indeed, the doctrine of the trinity was never without its critics—some of whom concluded that it was an a-rational doctrine that can only be accepted on faith. Whenever the history and teachings of the church were examined critically, the Doctrine of the Trinity was the place where the seams began to show. Whenever Christianity gave rise to a mystic vision of God, universalism was rediscovered, for the vision of mystic unity is inhospitable to a world -view which embraces the notion that some significant portion of creation is forever doomed to be excluded from that fundamental unity. Heretical though they may have been, anti-trinitarian and universalist thought never disappeared from the religious scene.

SERVETUS AND THE EARLY REFORMATION

When Martin Luther posted his ninety-five theses on the door of the castle church in Wittenberg in October 1517, he set off a sweeping re-examination of Christian teaching and practice that would eventuate in the Protestant Reformation. Luther's reformation was radical in its call for renewal of the church, in its determination to recover the authority of the Bible, in its rejection of the authority of the Pope. Calvinism would offer an even more radical alternative with its revision of the sacraments and its challenge to traditional church polity. Neither of these alternatives would be radical enough for some who would comprise the left wing of the Protestant Reformation. Not content to tinker around the edges, these reformers sought a reexamination of the fundamentals of Christianity. It was among these reformers that unitarianism and universalism would emerge, as the scriptures were searched, and individuals sought to be their own teachers and theologians.

The groundwork for the challenge to the Doctrine of the Trinity had been laid in the Nominalist thought of the late middle-ages. The Nominalists had argued that reality existed in concrete and specific things and that the classes by which we group things according to common properties have no existence apart from our own minds. Thus, there are chairs, but chairness, in which all chairs participate, does not exist. When extended to theology, nominalist thought suggested that a common substance shared by the three persons of the trinity is unreal. Only the three persons of the trinity exist, thus suggesting a tritheism. Since such a belief was counter to the teaching of the church, Nominalism had ended by insisting that the doctrine of the Trinity was irrational, and unprovable, and therefore must be accepted on the basis of faith, since the human mind could make no sense of it.

Additional challenge to the Doctrine of the Trinity, and even more, the partialist view of salvation, can be found in the mysticism of late medieval groups like the Brethren of the Common Life and others. Mysticism, rooted as it is in the personal experience of the holy, often has little patience with theological niceties. What is important for the mystic is the experience, not the explanation of the experience.

Those who have shared an experience of the immediate presence of the holy have an undeniable bond, regardless of the differences that may exist in their theological understandings of that experience. More than this, those who have experienced the sense of mystic unity as fundamental and undeniable reality, may have little enthusiasm for doctrines that exclude any part of creation from that unity. Finally, if one has had direct personal access to the holy, the role of the church and the priest as mediator may seem less necessary. Paradoxically, mysticism seems to engender both a deep concern for religion and a more casual response to the dictates of religious institutions.

Luther, in the early days of his revolt against the church in Rome, seemed more focused upon reforming corrupt practices than reforming doctrine. However, he soon discovered that these two concerns are not easily separable. His attack upon the practice of selling indulgences led him to seek revision of the theological assumption upon which that practice was based—the notion of a treasury of merit, accumulated by the saints, which the church could dispense at its discretion, and usually for a fee. Justification by faith alone is the theological response to the practice of indulgences. Reliance upon scripture is the theological response to those who quoted church tradition as a justification for practices which reformers regarded as corrupt.

It must be admitted, however, that Luther was not eager to tamper with the fundamental dogmatic structures of the church. He and his reform were dependent for their survival upon the good will of conservative princes. He could not afford to be seen as a wild-eyed radical willing to bring down the entire social edifice. There is some reason to think that Luther preferred to give little attention to some of the more debatable doctrines, including the Doctrine of the Trinity. This, after all, was one of those doctrines not well supported in scripture.[6] It is quite possible that Luther and the early reformers would have been content to remain silent on this doctrine—neither challenging it nor insisting upon it—had it not been for the Spanish theologian, physician, astrologer and editor Michael Servetus.

Servetus was born in Spain in 1511. The nature of his early education remains uncertain. He knew the Bible in Greek and Hebrew; he knew Latin, had an understanding of Scholastic philosophy, had read the church fathers, and was familiar with the Koran. At fifteen, he was a student of law in Toulouse.

In addition to formal education, Servetus was profoundly influenced by the world in which he grew up. Spain had been united only recently under the dual monarchy of Ferdinand and Isabella. In 1492, in addition to sending Columbus on his epochal voyage of discovery, Ferdinand and Isabella had sought to strengthen their hold on the Iberian Peninsula by driving into exile all non-Christians. Over eight hundred thousand Moslems and Jews left Spain in that year.

Others, not wanting to give up their homes and their livelihoods, converted to Christianity. Almost immediately, these converts were looked upon with suspicion. Was their conversion to Christianity the result of sincere conviction, or were they only pretending adherence to the faith, waiting for the moment when they might return safely to the faith of their ancestors? And if they were not sincere, might they not represent a threat to the nation in times of crisis?

These kinds of concerns resulted in the establishment of the Spanish Inquisition—an arm of the church charged with ensuring the orthodoxy of all who claimed to be Christian. Inevitably, the Inquisition found Moslems and Jews who practiced the Christian faith in public, but adhered to their ancient religious traditions and practices in private. Such people were jailed, tortured and sometimes burned in public as punishment for their deceitful behavior and as a warning to all who would, in any way, challenge the concept of one nation, one monarchy, one faith.

Growing up in the years after the expulsion of Jews and Moslems, Servetus was undoubtedly aware of the terrible fate awaiting those who were unable to embrace Christianity without reservation. Troubled by the on-going persecutions, he found himself wondering why, if Christianity be true, were people willing to risk prison, torture, the stake rather than embrace it whole-heartedly and abandon false religions completely. He came to the conclusion that the stumbling block for many was the Doctrine of the Trinity—a teaching of the church which seemed to many Jews and Moslems a violation of monotheism—a teaching which needed to be fully and carefully explained so that people could embrace it without hesitancy.

This concern led Servetus, while studying law in Toulouse, to begin a secret study of Scriptures and the writings of the early church fathers. Servetus discovered, to his great amazement, that the Doctrine of the Trinity has no firm support in the New Testament. This teaching for which men and women were being burned at the stake was nowhere spelled out in the teachings of Jesus or of the Apostles. What is more, the early church fathers seemed to know little or nothing of this central teaching of the church. Indeed, it was not until after 325 c.e. that speculation on and teaching about the Trinity begins to appear within the church. Men and women were being jailed and tortured and burned because they could not embrace a teaching about which the early church seemed to know nothing.

The result of his study was that Servetus became a radical religious reformer. His goal was to supplement the Lutheran reform by simplifying the teachings of the church, to restore the purity of doctrine, using as a standard of faith the early church as it existed before 325 c.e., and thus to make possible the true and complete conversion of Jews and Moslems.

While these ideas were taking shape in his mind, Servetus served as secretary to Juan de Quintana, court preacher to Charles V, the Holy Roman Emperor. In that capacity Servetus traveled to Italy for Charles' coronation in 1529. Here, his intellectual conviction that the church stood in dire need of reform was strengthened by deep shock at the worldliness of the church at its highest levels. Later he traveled to Augsburg with the court and on this journey met with several leading reformers. Eventually, he left the service of Quintana, though the reason and the date is uncertain. He traveled, meeting Oeclampadius, the reformer at Basel, and Erasmus, both of whom were unwilling to embrace the view Servetus put forward concerning further reformation of church teachings.

Disappointed by the response, Servetus distilled his findings and his concerns into a volume called ON THE ERRORS OF THE TRINITY. Here Servetus set forth his conviction that the Trinity is "a sterile doctrine which confuses the head and fails to warm the heart." In his system, Christ was fully human, and the Son of God, supernaturally begotten. For Servetus, Christ was God but not in the sense applied to the Father, and the Holy Spirit was to be understood as an activity of God. He believed a harmony of power but not of nature defined the relationship between Father, Son and Spirit.

This book, published in 1531, when Servetus was only 20, aroused a storm of controversy. The immediate consequence of its publication was that it embarrassed the reformers and forced them to a public discussion of issues they would rather have ignored. Ultimately, the book was banned at Strassburg and Servetus was denounced from the reformed pulpits in that city. Basel soon followed Strasburg's lead and the rest of the reformers quickly fell in line. The response to the book was almost universally hostile.

Feeling he had been misunderstood, Servetus tried again, publishing DIALOGUES ON THE TRINITY in which he tried to express his views while giving as little offense as possible. This effort resulted in additional harsh criticism from the leading reformers. On June 17, 1532, the Inquisition ordered his arrest and Servetus fled. A major consequence of Servetus' early work was that the Reformation, which, by and large, had avoided the doctrines that troubled him, now hastened to define itself in opposition to his radical criticism of doctrine.

Under an assumed name, Servetus established himself in Lyon, where he was employed by a publisher, as a proof reader and editor. In 1534 he was briefly at the University of Paris. Then he returned to Lyon, where he saw a new edition of Ptolemy's Geography through the press, and corrected proofs for medical treatises. Developing an interest in medicine he became a physician. Returning to Paris, he was embroiled in a controversy over astrology. He withdrew from Paris and moved to Vienne, where he established himself as a physician to the Bishop, living in the Bishop's palace. (At some point in his life, he discovered the circulation of blood through the lungs, anticipating the work of Harvey.)

Despite all his various successes, his old concern for theology would not be denied. His printer friend provided him with copies of the writings of John Calvin. This seemed to revive his dormant theological concern. In 1552, Servetus published CHRISTIANISMI RESTITUTIO, a work in which he argued that the church had fallen into false doctrine after 325 c.e. He insisted that the point of reformation should be to restore the church to its original purity of doctrine. He contended that Luther and the other reformers had not gone far enough in their reform of the Roman church. He insisted that the Trinity was a doctrine invented by Satan to confuse Christians and likened it to a three-headed Cerberus. He defined God as everywhere, the complete essence of all things. Betraying the influence of radical anabaptists, he insisted that baptism is to be understood as a sign of repentance and regeneration which, therefore, must be a conscious choice, and was not to be accepted before the twentieth, perhaps even the thirtieth year.

From Vienne, Servetus entered into correspondence with John Calvin, then at the height of his power in Geneva. At first Calvin seemed to believe his correspondent to be a sincere inquirer who might benefit from the reformer's careful instruction and correction. In time, Calvin found the correspondence growing tiresome as it became clear that Servetus was more interested in teaching than in being taught. Some of the correspondence began to grow abusive in tone—not unusual at the time.

Eventually a copy of the RESTITUTIO reached Calvin, who recognized it as the work of his mysterious correspondent. Someone in Geneva alerted the Inquisition that the author of this heretical volume was living in Vienne. Servetus was arrested and held in loose confinement. Arising early in the morning, and under the pretense of using the privy, Servetus escaped over the wall of the palace and fled the Inquisition a second time. He was convicted in absentia and sentenced to death. For four months, Servetus wandered through France. He seems to have been attempting to make his way into Northern Italy, by way of Geneva.

Recognized in Geneva, Servetus was arrested and charged with heresy. After a trial, in which Servetus was convicted, Calvin referred the case to the Swiss churches. They concurred in the finding of the court and recommended the harshest of punishments. In 1553, Michael Servetus was led from his cell, bound to a stake, and with his offending books strapped to his thigh, was burned to death and his ashes scattered.

Much of Europe applauded Calvin and Geneva. Some, however, were shocked and outraged and refused to join the general chorus. Sebastian Castellio, in Basel, wrote in protest. He argued that he was not a supporter of Servetus' views. Indeed, he insisted he never read them because Calvin burned the books along with their author. He reminded Calvin that no one in history had instituted more novelties of opinion and practice within Christendom than Calvin, himself, and therefore it little behooved him to burn a man for novel doctrine. He asked how burning a man defends a doctrine. "To burn a man," he insisted, "is not to defend a doctrine. It is to burn a man." Continuing the plea for tolerance, Castellio said:

> Christ's doctrine means loving one's enemies, returning good for evil, having a pure heart and a hunger and thirst for righteousness....Before God, and from the bottom of my heart I call you to the spirit of love.

> By the bowels of Christ, I ask and implore you to leave me in peace, to stop persecuting me. Let me have the liberty of my faith as you have of yours. At the heart of religion I am one with you. It is in reality the same religion; only on certain points of interpretation I see differently from you. *But however we differ in opinion, why cannot we love one an-*

other?...

There are, I know, persons who insist that we should believe even against reason. It is, however, the worst of all errors, and it is laid on me to fight it....*Let no one think he is doing wrong in using his mental faculties. It is our proper way of arriving at truth....*

My counsel is that thou cease to compel men's consciences, that thou cease to kill and to persecute, that thou grant to men who believe in Jesus Christ the privilege of serving God according to their own innermost faith and not according to some one else's faith. And you that are private people, do not be so ready to follow those who lead you astray and push you to take up arms and kill your brothers....

I am a poor little man, more than simple, humble and peaceable, with no desire for glory, only affirming what in my heart I believe. *Why cannot I live and say my honest word and have your love?*[1]

As the italicized sections indicate, in his response to the execution of Servetus, Castellio gave voice to the classic Unitarian insistence upon tolerance of diverse opinions, as well as the use of reason as the appropriate tool for arriving at religious convictions. Castellio insisted that there are two sources of knowledge—experience and revelation—and neither is above correction. When the two are in conflict, the arbiter must be human reason. Morality, he insisted, is to be found in loyalty to what one believes to be right, even if one is in error. He championed the primacy of conscience, insisting, "I must be saved by my own faith, and not that of another." In these sentiments, at least, Castellio is a fully modern religious liberal. Brought to trial for his writings, Castellio died in 1563, before the trial ended.

Servetus, by his dogged determination, had served to make the Doctrine of the Trinity a focus of discussion and concern for reformers who would rather have ignored this difficult and thorny teach-

ing. For much of the Radical Reformation it became a defining issue. His teachings on the Trinity are difficult and tortuous to the
modern mind. It is hard to imagine Servetus sitting comfortably
through a modern Unitarian Universalist service. Nonetheless, he
is part of the movement's mythic past and speaks across the centuries because of his stubborn refusal to be deflected from the truth as
he saw it, even though all the world disagreed. His death not only
gave Unitarians a martyr, but it provided the occasion on which
Castellio proclaimed the great commitment to reason and tolerance
in matters of religious conviction—a statement which makes him,
perhaps more than Servetus, the forerunner of modern Unitarian
Universalism.

There are those who insist that in significant ways, John Calvin
and his Reformed Church contributed more than Servetus to modern Unitarian Universalism. They argue that Lutherans remained
largely impervious to anti-trinitarian thought, while Calvinists
proved more susceptible and that as a consequence Unitarian Universalism has inherited much from the structure and practice of
Calvin's Reformed Church out of which it emerged. Whatever truth
there may be in this argument, it remains the fact that Unitarian
Universalists find it easier to identify with the martyrs than with
the persecutors. It is Servetus rather than Calvin who is honored,
and it is in Castellio's protest rather than Calvin's defense that Unitarian Universalists hear an echo of their own values.

ITALY AND THE RADICAL REFORMATION

Perhaps Michael Servetus risked discovery in Geneva—a place
he knew to be hostile to him—because it seemed to offer the best
and quickest route from France to Venice. He may have been seeking asylum in Northern Italy because, in the early years of the Reformation, a community of radical reformers had found refuge there.
In order to understand the emergence of Unitarianism in Poland
and Transylvania, we must explore the nature of the Radical Refor-

mation in Northern Europe, and its emergence in Italy.

When Luther nailed his ninety-five theses to the Chapel door in Wittenberg in 1517, his hammer-stroke wakened all kinds of slumbering resentments and discontents. Some were political and economic in nature. Others were doctrinal, rooted in the mystical speculations of the late middle-ages. While Luther had intended to focus on corrupt practices in the church, not its doctrines, it soon became clear that without the authority of the church as a standard, Protestants would have to establish some standard of their own. The classic Protestant appeal to scriptures only removed the question to another level, for the Bible, the Reformers would soon discover, is not self-explanatory, but always requires interpretation. Without a common standard of interpretation, each person became the final arbiter of meaning and doctrine. The consequence was that virtually every heresy which had ever troubled the church was now let loose upon the land.

Radical reformers, those who believed the magisterial reform of Luther represented only the beginning, often disagreed among themselves about the meaning of the Biblical texts and what they required. A quick survey can suggest some of the variety of the opinion that developed on Luther's left-flank. In 1524 several people were arrested in Nurnberg for teaching that there is only one God and Jesus is not that God. In 1527, Martin Cellarius published the first book to deny the special deity of Jesus. Cellarius insisted "Jesus is God; we are all God." Ludwig Haetzer was executed in 1529 for denying the doctrines of vicarious atonement, eternal punishment, and the trinity. Balthasar Hubmaier's NICKOLSBURG THESES (1527) taught that Christ was born in sin, that Mary was the mother of Christ but not of God, that Christ was a prophet, not God and his death did not atone for the sins of the world. Jacob Kautz taught universal salvation and regarded Christ as an example, not a savior. Johannes Campanus taught that God gave birth to the son who is neither equal nor eternal and that there is no third person in the trinity. Hans

Denck, a German mystic, insisted that religious truth is revealed by the inner word, and that the function of scripture is to confirm that inner word. For him the Trinity is defined as omnipotence, goodness and righteousness, while Christ functions as an example. In 1530, Conradin Bassen of Heilbronn was beheaded and burned for teaching that Christ is not our savior, was not god nor born of a virgin and for not believing in prayer, the New Testament or a future life.

The Radical Reformers shared a center of concern focused around the sacrament of baptism, a radical view of the nature of the church and the relation between church and state, and their understanding of the ultimate source of religious authority. For the most part, these reformers rejected infant baptism, insisting that admission to the church must reflect a conscious and responsible decision to conform one's life to the teachings of Christianity. Therefore, baptism, to have meaning, can only be offered to adults. Because the church must be a matter of personal choice, there must be a separation between church and state. If the two are not separate, the matter of choice for most people becomes moot. And finally, personal conviction, personal religious experience is the court of last resort. Like Luther, one must find the point of truth and stand upon it, though all the world disagree.

Out of these radical theological teachings, many of these reformers found in their reading of the scripture injunctions to radical social teachings as well. Some insisted that the New Testament clearly forbade any involvement by Christians in military service or in political life. Some preached equality of all Christians, insisting on communal property arrangements and even, in some cases, communal marriages. Some preached the imminent end of the world, urging Christians to abandon their worldly responsibilities in order to prepare themselves for the kingdom. Others insisted that Christians were obligated to engage in armed struggle against the forces of evil, sin and corruption and urged an uprising of peasants and the poor against their immoral, corrupt masters, and supported the peasants' revolt in Germany.

Much of this social radicalism came to focus in 1535 when Radical Reformers took over the city of Munster, expelled the Catholics and the Lutherans and set up their own theocracy. Catholics and Lutherans united to retake the city and expel the radicals, but the effect of the Munster experiment was to raise the level of anxiety among secular rulers, who instituted harsh and repressive measures against all appearance of radical thought. Between 1535 and 1546, some 30,000 followers of left-wing Protestantism were put to death in Holland and Friesland alone. The ferocity of the repression sent radical thinkers and their followers fleeing in all directions, many to Eastern Europe, some to Northern Italy.

Menno Simons, from whom modern Mennonites take their name, would eventually pull together the scattered remnants of this radical community, and provide a theological and organizational structure that would allow it to survive. The cost, however, would be high—a withdrawal from the world, and a lopping off of more extreme theological opinions. Among those driven from the community was Adam Pastor, the leader of the more liberal wing, who had taught that Christ is later in time and subordinate to God, and that prayers to Christ are inappropriate. Adam Pastor has been called the first real Unitarian in Europe.

Italian concern for reforming the Church was much less political in nature than was the German Reformation. Luther owed no small part of his success to the fact that his demand for a reformed church was made in the context of German resentment of what were perceived to be heavy and unfair financial demands from the Roman Church, and in a context of nascent nationalism which resented the influence of foreigners within the Germanies. From the days of Henry IV, at least, there had been a struggle between church and state, between pope and monarch. Luther had the good fortune to demand reform in a manner and at a time when these discontents could be wedded to his religious vision.

In Italy, the concern for reforming the church was far more influenced by the Renaissance, the rediscovery of ancient learning and the application of that learning to established doctrines and practices. For this reason, the Italian Reformation tended to emerge among the well educated and the well to do. As early as the mid 15th century, Italian intellectuals had been exploring Greek philosophy, and by the beginning of the 16th century, the influence of that exploration had given rise to informal communities, gathered to discuss topics of religious and philosophical concern. Within these communities there developed an interest in mystical experience, that truth which underlies all religious systems, even at the expense of weakening the claims of Christianity.

The most influential of these groups was the Neo-Platonic Academy that flourished in Naples between 1535 and 1541. Among the participants were Juan de Valdes (d.1541) and Bernardo Ochino, the most popular preacher in the Italy of his day. In his search for a truth beneath the dogmas, Valdes was led to question church teachings concerning vicarious atonement—the theory that in accepting death, Christ atoned for the sins of all humanity. During the years of the Academy, various participants would question the virgin birth, the divinity of Jesus, the resurrection, the trinity and other central dogmas of the Roman church.

Against this background of sophisticated skepticism and questioning, another version of Reformation emerged in Northern Italy, centered upon Venice. The Venetians were highly successful merchants with commercial ties to much of the known world. Their city was a sophisticated center of world travel and its citizens were accustomed to encountering diverse opinions and behaviors. The economic well being of the community was best served by a wide tolerance. What is more, Venetians had a highly developed resentment of Roman attempts to interfere in the affairs of their city. Given this environment, Venice became a haven for refugees from Northern

Europe, whose opinions and practices were anathema to Catholics and other Protestants as well.

As the number of religious radicals grew in and around Venice, their communities became centers where concern for reform of corrupt practices, which was the focus of the German Reformation, and concern for the reform of doctrine, which was the focus of the Italian Reformation, were merged into a radical, anti-trinitarian, anabaptist movement. As early as 1539, Servetus' books were circulating among these reformers and were being well received.

By mid century, congregations, meeting in sixty locations, were well organized, with a structure which included ordained ministers and visiting Bishops or Superintendents who had responsibilities beyond the local congregation. In 1550 they called a council (the Council of Venice) which adopted a statement of common beliefs. Each congregation was invited to send two delegates. Approximately sixty delegates attended, including representatives from groups in Switzerland and the Grisons[8]. The Council adopted a 10-point statement of faith, which said, among other things:

1. Christ is not God but man, born of Joseph and Mary, but filled with all the powers of God.

2. Mary had other sons and daughters after Christ.

3. There is no angelic being created by God but where Scripture speaks of angels it means men appointed by God for a given purpose.

4. There is no other Devil than human prudence, for no creature of God is hostile to him but this.

5. The wicked do not rise at the last day, but only the elect, whose head is Christ.

6. There is no hell but the grave.

7. When the elect die, they sleep until the judgment day, when all shall be raised.

8. The souls of the wicked perish with the body, as do all other animals.

9. The seed of man has from God the power of producing flesh and spirit.

10. The elect are justified by the eternal mercy and love of God without any outward work, that is, without the merits, the blood, or the death of Christ. Christ died to show forth the righteousness of God, that is, the sum of all the goodness and mercy of God and of his promises.[9]

The Roman Church, already struggling with insurrection in Germany, could ill afford to ignore the challenge in its own back yard. In 1542 the Inquisition was established in Italy. Almost immediately, the Neo-Platonic Academy, and other similar groups ceased to exist. Juan de Valdez had died in 1541, but Ochino was summoned to Rome. Warned that the summons was from the Inquisition, he fled Italy, making his way to Switzerland, where he became preacher to the Italian Congregation in Geneva—a congregation which worshiped in Italian, which was not closely watched by the other churches, and which became a seed-bed for various heresies until it was eventually brought to heel. Among those who escaped Italy in this period and were connected in one way or another with the Italian Congregation were Matteo Gribaldi, Giorgio Biandrata and Laelius Socinus.

In 1552, the Anabaptist community in Northern Italy was betrayed by one of its ministers, a former priest, who returned to the Roman Church and informed authorities of the teachings, practices, and secret meetings of the radical Protestants. The flourishing community was scattered. Some of its members recanted their heresies, some fled east, to Moravia or even Turkey, and some went underground. When he made the fateful decision that led him to Geneva, Servetus may have been unaware of the fate of the Anabaptist community in Northern Italy, or he may have hoped to find refuge among the Protestant underground.

For our story, one of the major figures to flee the Italian Inquisition in the middle of the sixteenth century was Laelius Socinus. Born in Sienna in 1525, and trained as a lawyer, Socinus moved to Venice when he was 21. His great passion was to relate human law to the law of god. This led him, inevitably, to a careful study of the scriptures. Like many of his contemporaries, Socinus came away from that study with a growing conviction that the teachings of the church were in fundamental conflict with scripture and with reason. That conviction was deepened and confirmed when he encountered the writings of Michael Servetus. In time, he abandoned the law and gave himself over entirely to the study of religion.

In 1547, Socinus left Italy for the Grisons, and then went on to Geneva and Basel. He was in England in 1548 where he met Bernardo Ochino, and then returned to the continent and to Geneva and Zurich. In 1551, he made a trip through Germany and on to Crakow in Poland, long a focus of Italian Culture, and then returned to Zurich. His travels made him acquainted with many of the major reformers, who seemed to regard him as a reverent skeptic, forever seeking the reason for doctrines before accepting them. For a time he lived with Castellio in Basel and may have collaborated with him on several works. He engaged in correspondence with Calvin. When Servetus was executed in 1553, Socinus was one of those who expressed disapproval. This made him suspect among the main-stream reformers. In response to this suspicion, he submitted a confession of faith for Bullinger, the reformer, a statement that has been described as filled with vague generalities clothed in orthodox terminology. After a brief trip to Italy, Laelius Socinus died in 1562, at the age of 37.

His estate consisted of little more than a trunk of books and manuscripts that contained the essence of his study and thought. The trunk was inherited by his nephew, Faustus Socinus. Faustus would study his uncle's legacy with care, and discover there the insistence that reason is equal to scripture in authority, a conviction which, when applied to church dogma would result in a revolution. In time, the reverent skepticism of Laelius Socinus, mediated and amplified by his more famous nephew, would become the basis of a religious movement in distant Poland.

POLISH SOCIANISM

Poland in the sixteenth century was the fourth largest power in Europe, covering a territory a little larger than modern Texas. The country was divided into three major regions, Great Poland to the west, Little Poland to the east, and the Duchy of Lithuania, which extended from the Baltic into modern Russia. The population of some 20 million, mostly peasants of Slavic descent, was primarily engaged in agriculture. Indeed, this peasant class was bound to the soil and enjoyed few if any rights. In the cities there were communities of German, Dutch and Scottish artisans and merchants. The dominant social class was the nobility, exempt from taxation, but required to provide military service to the state. In truth, at least half of the noble class was impoverished, but nonetheless the Polish nobility consisted of proud, strong-willed individualists, jealous of their rights and counted the best-educated, most highly cultivated nobility in Europe. At the apex of the social structure were the magnates, wealthy autocratic lords who monopolized public service, and were virtually sovereign on their great estates.

In 1519, Sigismund I of Poland married Bona Sforza, daughter of the Duke of Milan. The new queen brought with her to Poland a large entourage of Italians to function as servants and courtiers. From that moment on, Italian influence was strong in Poland, and was reflected in the arts, the literature, the architecture and the education of Poland's upper classes. A less beneficial import from Italy was simony—the selling of church offices to the highest bidder. This practice, begun in Poland under Bona's influence, would result in a weakening of respect for the Polish church.

History and geography shaped the religious situation in Poland. Geographically, Poland was on the fringes of Roman Catholic influence, and the roots of Roman Catholicism were shallow. The area had been converted relatively recently. (Poland became Christian in 965 c.e., and Lithuania as recently as 1386 c.e.) The authority of the Church of Rome had been accepted only slowly and reluctantly, the fiercely independent Poles being uneasy about foreign authority in their country, even in religious matters. What is more the Polish church could not help being affected by developments on its borders. Jan Huss and his followers had left a strong legacy among the Poles, suggesting that the Roman Church was not beyond challenge. And, of course, being a frontier state, Poland had learned a degree of tolerance for Roman Catholics, Greek Orthodox, Jews and Moslems.

By the end of the fifteenth century, the Roman Church had little real hold in Poland and only modest influence in its churches. The Polish church had grown wealthy and lax. A significant number of the clergy was married. The king had wrested away the power to name the Bishops. What is more, few seemed to care about the condition of the church or its teachings. Indeed, the Bishop of Crakow is quoted as saying, "Believe in a goat if you like, provided you pay me my tithes."[10]

The weakening of ecclesiastical authority was matched by a weakening of secular government as well. After 1572, the monarchy became an elected office, the king chosen by the Diet. The government consisted of a senate of 139 members, including representatives of the church, which had a largely advisory function and a Diet of 200 members of the lesser nobility. The Diet operated on the basis of the "free veto" which allowed any member to block action by the body. What is more, even when the Diet was able to reach agreement, the estates of the great nobles were inviolable. Thus, sympathetic nobles were able to provide sanctuary from inconvenient laws and edicts.

When the Reformation broke over Northern Europe, it was inevitable that it would find a welcome in Poland. The Lutheran version of the Reformation established itself in Prussia, Great Poland

and Little Poland, while the Bohemian Brethren, followers of the Hussite Reform, were to be found in Great Poland. The Calvinist or Reformed Church would be centered in Little Poland and Lithuania.

The early Reformation swept into the country unofficially, with dissident groups meeting in private homes, especially in the halls of nobles where they would be safe from molestation. In those early years the support of the nobility was essential to the progress of reform, since the attitude of the monarchy was less than enthusiastic. Recognizing the strength of the nobility, Sigismund I reluctantly chose not to oppose the Reformation openly, insisting that he "preferred to be king of the sheep and the goats."[11] When he died in 1548, a reaction set in under his successor, Sigismund Augustus.

In 1550, Nicholas Olesnicki drove out the monks from a monastery on his lands, and established a reformed church. The Bishops, over-reaching themselves, sought to retaliate and at a synod in 1552 urged that the death penalty be used to combat the growing heresy in the land. Alarmed by what seemed a challenge to their rights, the Polish nobility united to defend their prerogatives against the power of the church. In 1553 Prince Nicholas Radziwill lead the Duchy of Lithuania into the Reformed Church. The result was that Protestantism in its various forms became tolerated, de facto, within the boundaries of Poland and Lithuania.

In 1555, the Polish Diet decreed freedom of religion to commoners and nobles alike, and that same year the Polish Reformers joined with the Bohemian Brethren in a federation of the two bodies. The weakness of the central government, the weakness of the established church and the independence of the nobility had worked to make Poland something of a haven for Protestants. These conditions, combined with the strong Italian influence present within the country, drew to Poland Italian anabaptist and humanist reformers fleeing persecution elsewhere in Europe.

The importance of this connection for the history of the Reformed Church in Poland can be seen in the fact that the Superintendent of the Reformed Church, one Dr. Francesco Lismanino, had been confessor to Queen Bona. She, in turn, had given Lismanino, along with various other Protestant works, books of sermons by Bernardo Ochino. In 1551, when Laelius Socinus visited Poland, he met and talked with Lismanino. Two years later, Lismanino travelled to Switzerland, returning to Poland in 1556. In his absence, Jan Laski had been busily organizing new Reformed Congregations. By the time of Laski's death in 1560, there were 160 Reformed Congregations in the country.

It was within these Reformed Congregations that anti-trinitarian thought would develop and spread through Poland and Lithuania. The seed of this heresy had been planted decades earlier. In 1539, one Catherine Weigel, aged 80, was burned at the stake for refusing to believe Christ was the Son of God. It is not clear precisely the nature of her heresy; there is some thought she may have been a convert to Judaism. But in the popular mind, at least, her death was the result of a challenge to the doctrine of the trinity.

In 1546, a group of humanists, meeting for discussion of theological concerns, was visited by a stranger known only as "Spiritus."[12] Whoever he may have been, Spiritus challenged the conventional wisdom of the day by suggesting that the Doctrine of the Trinity represents, in fact, a form of polytheism, the worship of three gods. Among those in attendance at this meeting was Francesco Lismanino, who would later become Superintendent of the Reformed Churches in Poland. The doubts planted in his mind, and the minds of others would grow quietly until, in time, they would shatter the unity of the Reformed churches in Poland.

In time, the issue of the Doctrine of the Trinity became sufficiently disturbing so that questions concerning it and other doctrinal matters were referred to the Reformed churches in Switzerland, but that would not lay the issue to rest. In 1556, at the Synod of Secemin, Peter Gonesius, a client of Nicholas Rasziwill, raised the issue of the trinity anew. Gonesius had been in Italy at the time of

Servetus' death. He had returned to Poland by way of Moravia and the anabaptist communities there. He had come to embrace the social views, including the pacifism, of the Moravian Brethren. At the synod, he argued, among other things, that the scriptures offer the only standard of faith, that the Father is the only God, that only God deserves worship, that Christ is not the same as God. After two days of debate, Gonesius' opinions were rejected and he was expelled. But this first public debate of the trinity in Poland set a number of nimble minds to thinking. In time, of the sixteen ministers present at the debate, seven would end up in the anti-trinitarian camp.

Rejected by the synod, Gonesius returned to Lithuania where he worked to create an anti-trinitarian movement. He received strong support from ministers and nobles alike, who gave him aid and protection. Here he raised questions about the validity of infant baptism, and sought to establish the connection between religion and the social issues of the day. In the process, he gradually out-grew his Arian Christology and moved toward a Unitarian position. In many ways, he staked out the territory that the anti-trinitarian movement in Poland would occupy.

Having met the challenge on the left, the Reformed Church in Poland now found itself confronted on the right by Francesco Stancaro, who has been called the most disagreeable theologian in history. He had quarreled with the Lutherans, with the Poles, the Transylvanians and the Hungarians. A strict trinitarian, he was determined to root out any remaining vestiges of Arian thought in the Polish Reformed Church. The focus of his concern was over the role of Christ as mediator. Stancaro insisted that Christ was, in all ways, co-equal with God. However, he acknowledged that Christ functioned as God's mediator with humanity and that a mediator, by nature, must be inferior. Therefore, he concluded that only Christ's human nature could be involved in mediation, because if it were otherwise, then Christ's divine nature would have to be inferior to the Father's. In response, Lismanino, not wanting to endorse a separation between the human and the divine in Christ, insisted on the superiority, or at least the preeminence of the Father within the trinity. He argued that God and Christ are one, but that Christ is somewhat inferior to God the Father, thus falling dangerously close to an Arian position regarding the Christ. Ultimately, Stancaro would be excommunicated.

It is at this point, in 1558, that Giorgio Biandrata returned to Poland from Switzerland, accompanied by Laelius Socinus. Biandrata is one of the central figures in the development of antitrinitarian thought in Eastern Europe. Born in 1515, Biandrata was a physician specializing in women's diseases. In 1540 he was appointed court physician to Bona Sforza, Queen of Poland. (Subsequently, he would fill the same role for Bona's daughter, Isabella, the widow of John Zapolya, prince of Transylvania at the time when Unitarianism was emerging in that region.) In 1551, Biandrata returned to Italy, where he fell under the influence of the Reformation. In 1556, he fled Italy and like many others, sought refuge from the Inquisition in Geneva, where he became a member, indeed an Elder of the Italian Congregation.

While a member of that congregation, Biandrata was involved in discussions concerning the deity of Christ and the doctrine of the Trinity. He took his questions and concerns directly to John Calvin, who responded patiently, but was unable to satisfy Biandrata. Eventually Calvin lost patience, concluding that Biandrata was not a sincere seeker of truth and spiritual enlightenment, but rather a determined trouble-maker. Calvin's attention was drawn to the Italian Congregation and the heretical discussions that were the intellectual fare of the émigrés. Calvin, fearing that the Italian Church had become a seed-bed of the very heresies for which Servetus had been burned, determined to impose a more orthodox confession of faith on the Congregation.

Feeling the climate of opinion growing less friendly, Biandrata chose to leave Geneva and seek a new home in Zurich. Accompanying him was one Gianpaolo Alciati, also a member and a deacon of the Italian Congregation. Some hint of the opinions of Biandrata and Alciati might be gained from Alciati's insistence that "In the Trinity we worship three devils, worse than all the idols of the papacy, because we make it three persons." Biandrata was soon ordered to leave Zurich. Accompanied by Socinus, he traveled to Poland where he would be joined by Alciati, whose property had been confiscated, and who had been banished from Geneva.

Biandrata and Laelius Socinus arrived in Poland in 1558, in the midst of the debate over the doctrine of the Trinity engendered by Stancaro. Biandrata argued for tolerance within the church, and recommended that henceforth discussion of the disputed doctrine should abandon reliance on the terms derived from philosophy and theology and rest instead on the language of the Gospels and the Apostles' Creed. This suggestion appears quite reasonable until it is remembered that the doctrine of the Trinity developed only after 325 c.e., and therefore, has little or no support in the Gospels, the Epistles or the early church fathers. The effect of Biandrata's suggestion would be to strip supporters of the doctrine of the Trinity of any language with which to advance or defend it.

Returning from a visit to Transylvania, Biandrata, despite Calvin's warning to the Reformed Church concerning the Italian's theological unorthodoxy, was elected Co-adjutor of the reformed churches. In that position, Biandrata sought to focus the attention and the energies of the churches on ethical concerns and educational issues rather that on theological divisions. More conservative members of the clergy, however, remained suspicious of the Italian physician.

In 1561, Calvin's charges against Biandrata became public. In response, Biandrata was examined and found to be free of heresy. The same year a book by Giovanni Gentile, attacking the Athanasian Creed, appeared in Poland and Lismanino found himself accused of tampering with the doctrine of the Trinity. Biandrata once more urged conciliation, suggesting that one ought not coerce the conscience on matters where the scriptures are unclear. The orthodox churchmen, under Stanislas Sarniki, responded by seeking support from Calvin and other more orthodox reformers.

In 1562, the Synod reaffirmed Biandrata's orthodoxy, called on Calvin to be reconciled to the Italian physician, and renewed the admonition that ministers should avoid philosophical terms concerning the Trinity and confine themselves to the Gospels, the Apostles and the Apostles' Creed in seeking the language with which to discuss doctrine.

Frustrated in the attempt to force a break with Biandrata, Sarniki and the conservatives responded with an attack on Gregory Paulus, the distinguished minister of the congregation in Crakow, accusing him of being unsound on the Trinity. In August of 1562, they maneuvered Paulus into asserting the strict Unity of God. As a consequence, Paulus was removed from the church at Crakow. He and his followers established a new congregation at a new site. Sarniki, later that year, organized a separate synod of the more conservative preachers.

Given the division of the Reformed Church into two bodies, Biandrata invited anti-trinitarian Italians to Poland. In response, Alciati and Gentile joined forces with the congregations that looked to Gregory Paulus as their leader. In 1563, Biandrata was called to Transylvania. A year later the Calvinist reaction began to gather force, at the same time as the Catholic reaction to the Reformation began under Cardinal Hosius and the Jesuits. Both sought to use the power of the state to crush the liberals; the King responded in 1564 with an edict that banished all foreign born anti-trinitarians from Poland. The following year the anti-trinitarians made one last effort at harmony with the more orthodox members of the Reformed Church. With the failure of that attempt, the two groups began their separate histories.

The anti-trinitarian congregations are described as "the brethren in Poland and Lithuania who have rejected the Trinity." Their opponents called them "Arians;" they called themselves "Christians." In history they are known as the Minor Reformed Church of Poland, or the Polish Brethren, or later, and most often, as Socinians. The Minor Church of Poland included within its congregations the best-educated, strongest elements of the Reformed Church. After 1565, rejection of the trinity was a commonly accepted position among them. However, there was disagreement on a number of other issues.

If all agreed that Christ was not equal with God, it was not at all clear just what the relation of Christ to God might be and whether or not prayers and worship should be directed to Christ. Nor was it clear what to make of the Holy Spirit. But most divisive was the issue of baptism.

Influenced by the Anabaptists, some argued that since baptism was a sign of admission into the Christian community, and since participation in that community requires a conscious choice, baptism should be reserved for adults. Infant baptism, they argued, is invalid, and therefore, those who have been baptized as infants must be rebaptized upon admission to the church. Others insisted upon the necessity of their children being baptized so that they might grow up within the Christian community. There was much debate, and in the face of threatened schism, the synod resolved that each person must be guided by the Holy Spirit, that no one should be forced against conscience, and that all should dwell together in peace until the next synod. Subsequent synods ended with the participants giving and accepting forgiveness for any offense, and promising to live in peace together. Thus, tolerance of differences became an institutionalized custom among the Polish Brethren. In time, infant baptism would die out among them, without schism and without liberty of conscience being compromised.

The political situation in Poland in the late 1560's was complicated by the recognition that the King would soon die without leaving an heir. The Diet would be called upon to elect a new monarch for a recently united Poland and Lithuania. In some ways, this would be a crucial moment for the religious communities in the nation. The Protestants felt a need to present a common front if they were to work out an accommodation with the Catholics. In 1570, the Lutherans, the Calvinists and the Bohemian Brethren created the Union of Sandomir in order to be able to defend themselves and present a strong case to the new monarch.

The Union of Sandomir deliberately excluded the Minor Church. In response, the Polish Brethren sought support from the Moravian Brethren, an anabaptist group quite similar in social composition to the Polish Brethren. However, the theological differences were too great for any kind of union to be consummated between these two communities. The Minor Church found itself isolated and without political support at a crucial moment.

In 1569, Jan Sieninski, whose wife was "an Arian," had established the town of Rakow on the basis of broad religious toleration. To this new town anti-trinitarians soon flowed, hoping to create an ideal community. All classes in the town were expected to work, but the real focus of the community was on religious discussions. The most extreme social and theological views were aired within the community, which has been described as a perpetual synod. When the minister of the town resigned, he was not replaced, leaving the church at Rakow in the hands of lay leaders. Eventually, the chaos of its religious life threatened the existence of the town and so the church was reorganized in 1572, and for some 60 years thereafter Rakow served as the capital of Polish Unitarianism. From its press, books poured forth in a steady stream. Its public library was renowned. Its school attracted students from all over Europe, and enrolled one thousand students in its five-year program. The focus of its life and the test of Christianity in Rakow was understood to be the Sermon on the Mount.

The childless King of Poland died in 1572. His successor, elected by the Diet in 1573, was required to swear an oath of religious toleration, the Pax Dissidentium, pledging the King, as a condition of his accession to the throne, to preserve the peace and not interfere in religious matters. The new ruler, Stephen Bathori, a soldier much involved in wars, had little time for public controversy. Nonetheless, he was a staunch Catholic, and within the limits of his coronation oath, supported the Catholic revival in his Kingdom.

This decade in the life of the Minor Church was filled with a variety of controversies. Theologically, the church was split on the issue of whether it is appropriate to pray to and worship Jesus. The Poles, closer in spirit to German anabaptists, argued that Jesus was mediator and intercessor and therefore prayers and worship directed toward him were appropriate. The Lithuanians, closer in spirit to Transylvanian Unitarians, argued that only God deserved prayer and worship.

At the same time, the old social issues began to reappear. As Poland mobilized in the face of threatened war, the Polish Brethren found themselves forced to decide anew whether a Christian can participate in the military, or even in the government. They also debated the appropriateness of swearing oaths, of owning serfs, of owning any property. And all of this dissention grew as the early leaders of the Minor Church were passing from the scene. Without strong leadership, the Minor Church of Poland was falling into disrepair.

At this critical juncture, Faustus Socinus arrived on the scene. Faustus was the nephew of Laelius Socinus, and the heir to his uncle's trunk full of manuscripts. He had been involved with Protestant communities in Lyon, Geneva, Basel and Florence. In 1578, building on the thought of his uncle, he wrote a work entitled DE JESU CRISTO SERVATORE, in which he had argued that Jesus is the savior not because he suffered the death which human beings deserved, but because he showed in his life and death the path to salvation. Salvation comes by imitation of the life of Christ, not as the result of some divine scheme to pay an infinite debt. The focus of the religious life for Socinus was not correct doctrine but correct living.

Though the book was not published until 1594, it circulated in manuscript form, and came to the attention of Biandrata, who invited its author to Transylvania to assist in a debate over worship of Christ. In 1579, responding to the invitation, Faustus Socinus traveled to Transylvania by way of Crakow and while in that city visited the Minor Church and engaged its leaders in discussion.

In 1580, Socinus returned to Poland where he would spend the rest of his life. He associated himself with the congregation of the Minor Church in Crakow. It is interesting to note that Faustus Socinus would never become a member of the religious community to which he gave his name. The church in Crakow insisted on adult baptism; Socinus regarded this demand as unreasonable. Therefore, he was never admitted to the "Lord's Supper." In all other areas he participated fully in the life of the congregation, and eventually would provide the focus, the theological structure, the leadership that would define the Minor Church of Poland.

As we have suggested, Socinus arrived at a moment when a leadership vacuum had appeared, and when a dangerous social and political situation demanded that the Minor Church clarify its beliefs and its response to the world. Socinus sided with those who insisted that it was proper and appropriate to address prayers and worship to Jesus as mediator, thus halting the dangerous "Judaizing trend" which might have made the Minor Church even more vulnerable in a hostile political climate.

In dealing with social issues, Socinus insisted that the command not to kill is clear and without exception for Christians. Therefore, Christians could not engage in warfare or in any activity that might cause them to take a life. Nor was the punishment of criminals a Christian office. However, Christians were also citizens of the commonwealth, and as such must be obedient to government and to pay all just taxes. What is more, Christians had an obligation to serve in public office, provided only that the office did not require the imposition of the death penalty. And as citizens, Christians were permitted to defend themselves in courts of law.

Jesuits and other critics insisted that by refusing to accept an obligation to support the nation when it was at war, Socinus was undermining the authority of the King and the security of the state. So hostile was the reaction that Socinus left Crakow and spent four years in refuge. Those four years were spent in writing, providing counsel to the church, and debating with orthodox critics. It was during this same period that Socinus married.

At the end of four years, Socinus returned to Crakow, the acknowledged leader of the Minor Church, and the focus of antagonism for all who opposed its teachings. Shortly after the return to Crakow, Socinus' wife gave birth to their daughter, and then died of a recurrent illness. At the same time, his property in Italy was seized by the Inquisition, leaving Socinus poverty-stricken and dependent upon the charity of others. Despite these blows, he continued as the champion of the Minor Church in their debates with the Jesuits. His position caused him to be attacked frequently in print, and in 1594, he was physically attacked in the streets by Catholic soldiers. In 1598 he was attacked by a mob of Catholic students, who dragged him from his sick bed, burned his books and papers, and would have drowned him had he not been rescued by a university professor.

In 1601, his health failing, Socinus convened a meeting at Rakow with twelve leading ministers of the Minor Church. For three weeks the group engaged in discussion of important doctrinal concerns and social issues. In 1602, a second such meeting was held, in which Socinus defended the right of Christians to own property and to receive interest, while opposing luxury and greed. Once again, he functioned to moderate the extreme positions within the church and to preserve the church from division.

Knowing his time to be short, Socinus also began to collect and revise his works. Following his death on March 3, 1604, the church began a systematic publication of his writings. For the next quarter century there would be a steady stream of Socinian thought from the press at Rakow, making Socinianism an enduring factor in the religious thought of Western Europe. The complete works were published in 1668 at Amsterdam, in the collection know as THE LIBRARY OF THE POLISH BRETHREN.

At the time of Socinus' death the Minor Church seemed well established. In 1600 there were three hundred congregations. Over 500 titles had come off the press at Rakow. Local and general synods were held regularly for rational debate and discussion of religious issues, and scholars and missionaries were sent throughout Europe spreading the Socinian faith to susceptible minds in many parts of the continent.

In 1605, the Minor Reformed Church of Poland issued the Racovian Catechism, a text that set forth the positions of the church in a form which could be used for teaching. While stating the doctrines of the church, it placed heavy stress on moral life and the duties and responsibilities of a true Christian. It is striking because it presents scripture, reason and humanist thought as equally important authorities in religious matters. Despite the fact that the Catechism would be burned in England in 1614, it remained in print and in use for two hundred years.

Nor was the hostility to Socinian thought confined to England. Pressure on the Minor Church of Poland grew steadily through the years, forcing the Socinians to continue to seek allies among the liberal Calvinists in Holland, the Mennonites in Danzig and elsewhere. None of these efforts proved successful in relieving the unremitting pressure from Protestants and Catholics alike.

When the Jesuits succeeded in convincing Sigismund III that a promise made to heretics need not be kept, and therefore his coronation oath was not binding, the pressures on all Protestants began to build, but the full consequences fell first on the Minor Church as the smallest, weakest, most isolated. The church in Lublin was destroyed, its congregation banned. Lay members were arrested, fined, and in some cases executed. And then, in 1638, Rakow was lost.

The crisis at Rakow began with a quarrel over a boundary. A neighbor had erected a crucifix near the boundary of what he insisted was his land. Students at the Racovian school had stoned it and broken it down. The Racovians apologized and sought to make amends, but the Diet demanded an investigation, which ended with an order to close the school, abolish the press and banish all "Arians" from Racow. The Minor Church established a new center at Kisielin which was closed six years later. A new center was established at Luckawice near the Hungarian border.

Between the years 1642 and 1662, the Socinians were in constant controversy with the Jesuits, who charged the Socinians with Devil worship. The Minor Church mustered its strength to respond, but with no press to publish their arguments, the effort was not effective. Then war completed what the Jesuits had started. In 1648, the Cossack Wars destroyed the center of Socinianism, and half of all the Socinian churches in Little Poland. Six years later, war with Russia destroyed the churches in Lithuania. When Charles X of Sweden invaded in 1655, the Polish King vowed that if he were able to defeat the invaders, he would extend the worship of the Virgin throughout the nation, would lift the oppression of the peasants, and would banish the Arians from the realm.

In 1660, a successful Jan Casimir kept his vow regarding the Arians. The Socinians were ordered to leave Poland. Despite courageous and heroic attempts by leaders of the Minor Church, led by Socinus' grandson, Andrew Wiszowaty, to reverse the order, it became effective on July 10, 1660. The Socinians fled to Prussia, to the Rhine Palatinate, to Holstein, to Brandenburg, to Holland and to Transylvania. One thousand families remained in Poland, practicing their faith in secret, served by visiting preachers—Wiszowaty among them—who, for years, would make the dangerous trip back to their homeland on a regular basis to succor the faithful.

The history of the Minor Church of Poland came to an end, presaging the destruction of all of Protestantism within Poland. The legacy of the Socinian movement, its message of reason and tolerance, its insistence that religion is more a matter of right living than of right doctrine was scattered across Europe, like seed waiting for the season of growth and renewal.

TRANSYLVANIAN UNITARIANISM

Transylvania is a region two-thirds the size of the state of Maine. Currently, most of Transylvania is contained within the boundaries of Romania. Historically, it constituted a major trade route from Asia and the east into Europe. In Roman times it was the province of Dacia. After the fall of Rome, the geography which had made it a trade route also made it a path for barbarian invasions of the west. The Goths, the Huns, the Gepidae, the Avars, the Lombards, the Magyars, the Tartars and the Turks, in successive waves, entered Europe through Transylvania. After the Turks captured Constantinople, much of the trade dried up, leaving Transylvania an isolated backwater. In the sixteenth century, it comprised the eastern quarter of the Kingdom of Hungary under its own Count or Vaivode until 1556, when Transylvanians achieved a precarious independence.

Transylvania was a patchwork country consisting of a number of ethnic groups living side by side with little interaction. The "three united nations of Transylvania" consisted of the Szeklers, the Magyars and the Saxons. The Szeklers were a people of uncertain origin, though some claimed they were descended from pockets of settlers left behind by the Huns as they retreated from Europe after the death of Attila. Considered nobility, the Szeklers were exempt from taxes in exchange for their service in guarding the border region. The Szeklers were largely confined to the four eastern counties. The Magyars, who dominated Hungary and the eight Northern and Western Counties of Transylvania, were, because of geography, more influenced by Western culture and foreign influences. The Saxons were descendents of Germans who had been invited to settle in Transylvania by Geza II of Hungary, in the twelfth century, and who had maintained their own ethnic and cultural identity and close contacts with their land of origin.

In addition to these three major groups, there were a number of so-called "tolerated nations" in Transylvania. Among these were the Wallachs, the poorest part of the population, serfs and peasants with no political rights, largely Orthodox in their religion; Gypsies who appeared in Transylvania about 1523, their origins shrouded in mystery to this day; Jews, Armenians and a half dozen other small groups.

Like Poland, Hungary, which included Transylvania until 1556, existed on the fringes of Roman influence, indeed on the fringes of Europe. The region had been converted only in 1000 c.e., and its geography brought it into constant contact with Greek Orthodox, Islamic and Jewish influences. Much of its history in the sixteenth century was shaped by the on-going confrontation between the Islamic forces of the east and the Christian forces of the west. Indeed, it was as a consequence of that struggle that Transylvania was able to assert and maintain a period of independence in the second half of that century.

In 1526, in the battle of Mohacs, the armies of the Turkish Empire decisively defeated the Hungarian army. In the battle, King Louis II and most of the nobility and leadership of Hungary were killed. Two candidates, John Zapolya of Transylvania and Ferdinand of Austria, sought the vacant throne. A Diet at Szekesfehervar in Transylvania unanimously chose John as King of Hungary. Ferdinand was elected King by a German dominated Diet at Pozsony. The inevitable result was civil war.

In the course of the struggle, John was defeated and fled to Poland. From exile, he appealed to the Sultan for aid. The Sultan, preferring John's policy of independence for Hungary to Ferdinand's policy of an alliance with the west, invaded and drove Ferdinand to Vienna. John was restored to the throne, but the civil war dragged on for ten years. Eventually the two rivals, worn out in a struggle neither could win, agreed to a peace treaty in 1538.

By the terms of the treaty, John would remain King of Hungary and keep Transylvania and that part of Hungary he held at the time the treaty went into effect, while Ferdinand would retain control of the territory already in his hands. If John were to die without issue, Ferdinand would inherit all his lands. If John produced a son to succeed him, the son would inherit his father's hereditary possessions, i.e. Transylvania, but would not succeed to the throne of Hungary.

Subsequently, John Zapolya married Isabella, the daughter of Sigismund I and Bona of Poland. A year later, John fell seriously ill. While on his sick bed he learned that his wife had given birth to a son, John Sigismund. Within two weeks of the birth, John Zapolya died. However, he had used those two weeks well. He had appointed two crafty and able counselors, George Martinuzzi and Peter Petrovics, and charged them to secure the crown for his son. In addition, he had commended Isabella to the Sultan. Immediately upon the death of Zapolya, the infant son was crowned King of Hungary and Queen Isabella and the two counselors were named regents. At once, Ferdinand invaded, but was driven off by the Sultan's army, while the Queen and the young King moved to Gyulafehervar, the capital of Transylvania.

In 1543, Transylvania declared its independence and the following year the Diet recognized John Sigismund as King and his mother, Isabella, as Queen, although much of the power remained in the hands of the Queen's advisor, George Martinuzzi. In 1544, Queen Bona of Poland sent her trusted physician, Giorgio Biandrata, to Transylvania, to attend her daughter, Isabella, and her grandson, John Sigismund. From that moment, Biandrata would function as a trusted advisor and counselor to the Queen and her son.

Unable to force the issue by military means, Ferdinand resorted to more subtle methods. He offered Martinuzzi an archbishopric and a cardinal's hat in exchange for betraying Isabella. Alerted to the plot, Isabella fled with her son to Poland. In her entourage was Giorgio Biandrata. In time, Martinuzzi became archbishop and cardinal, but eventually he died at the hands of Ferdinand's soldiers. The Sultan, in the meantime, refused to accept the result of Martinuzzi's treachery. He warned Ferdinand that he would not make peace unless Isabella were restored to the throne of an independent Transylvania, and threatened an immediate invasion. Ultimately, Ferdinand acceded to the Sultan's demand. Isabella and the Prince were recalled in 1555, and returned the following year. It was in the context of this political turmoil that the Reformation took root in Transylvania.

It must be noted that the history of this region is dotted with heterodoxy. The earliest missionaries in the area had been Arian Christians sent by the emperor Valens. Bishop Ulfilas, who translated the New Testament into Gothic, and who was the founder of Gothic Literature, was an Arian. Consequently, the Goths had been Arian in their theology. Attila, in his passage through the region had favored Arianism. Indeed, Arianism remained strong throughout the area through the tenth century, and while there is no direct connection between that early religious thought and later Unitarianism, this history of Transylvanian heterodoxy may have made heresy seem less strange. What is more, on the eve of the Reformation, the influence of the Roman Church was less strong than in the nations of Western Europe. For example, the Inquisition never exercised any control in Hungary and Hungarians had never paid tithes to Bishops or to Rome.

The Reformation entered Transylvania early, by way of the Saxons, who imported Luther's writings before 1520. A royal decree, designed to secure the support of the Holy Roman Emperor against the Turks, was issued in 1523, outlawing heretics. However, the political situation was too unstable to allow the government to muster the resources to enforce its edict. What is more, the territories controlled by the Turks offered a constant nearby refuge for Protestants of various stripes, fleeing persecution.

After the disaster at Mohacs, the rival kings, John and Ferdinand, both staunch Catholics, opposed the spread of Lutheranism, but neither could muster the necessary resources to halt its spread. The German towns became Lutheran shortly after 1529. Soon the Magyars and the Szeklers followed suit. The Lutheran churches were organized into German and Hungarian sections under the supervision of a single Bishop. The Roman Catholic Bishop fled from Transylvania and most Catholic officials and gentry soon joined him in exile. There would not be another Catholic Bishop in Transylvania for 150 years, and only eight noble families and three magnates in the country remained loyal to their Catholic tradition.

In the period of time that lapsed between the recall of Queen Isabella and the Prince in 1555 and their return to Transylvania in 1556, the Regent was Peter Petrovics, a Calvinist Protestant. He used the interval to advance the reform of the Church. Priests were turned out; images were torn down; sacred vessels were melted down and minted into coinage. A meeting of the Diet in November of 1555 took formal measures to advance the new faith.

By the time Isabella returned to Transylvania, the Reformation was too well established to be uprooted. She responded to the religious situation by decreeing toleration for Calvinism and Lutheranism. Then, in 1557, in response to a request of the Diet meeting at Torda, the Queen decreed:

> Inasmuch as We and Our Most Serene Son have assented to the most instant supplication of the Peers of the Realm, that each person maintain whatever religious faith he wishes, with old or new rituals, while We at the same time leave it to their judgment to do as they please in the matter of faith,

just so long, however, as they bring no harm to bear on anyone at all, lest the followers of a new religion be a source of irritation to the old profession of faith or become in some way injurious to its followers—therefore, Peers of the Realm, for the sake of procuring the peace of the churches and of stilling the controversies that have arisen in the gospel teaching, we have decreed to establish a national synod, wherein, in the presence of devoted ministers of the Word of God as well as of other men of rank, genuine comparisons of doctrine may be made and, under God's guidance, dissensions and differences of opinion in religion may be removed.[13]

In view of the intolerance of dissent displayed throughout Europe at the time, this edict is a remarkable document, designed to protect minority opinions and to keep the peace.

Despite her attempts to establish peace and tolerance within the realm, Isabella was not popular with her subjects. Her efforts to reach a settlement with Ferdinand were viewed with suspicion. She found herself the constant focus of plots. Isabella died in 1559, leaving the throne to her son, John Sigismund, who was nominally the King of Hungary, but whose authority extended over little more than Transylvania.

The effect of the edict of Torda was to make possible public discussion and debate of the many issues that had been raised by the Reformation. As early as 1550, the debate between the Lutherans and the Calvinists over the meaning of the Lord's Supper had spread east to Hungary. (Lutherans insisted that the real presence of Christ was to be found in the elements of the Communion, while Calvinists insisted that the observance was a symbolic act of remembrance.) By 1556, Calvinism was stirring in Transylvania. At the outset, the Calvinists were condemned because of their extreme iconoclasm, which violated the spirit of the Edict of Torda. Eventually, as they became less extreme, the Calvinists would be included within its circle of protection.

Central to the emergence of Unitarianism within the Reformed Church in Transylvania is David Ferencz, known to the western world as Francis David. Born at Kolozsvar in 1510, Francis David was the son of a Saxon shoemaker father and a Magyar mother from a noble family, a remarkable heritage in a country where the crossing of ethnic boundaries was neither customary nor frequent. By the nature of his family situation, David grew up fluent in German and in Hungarian. From 1545-1548, he was a student at Wittenberg.

On his return to Transylvania, Francis David was made rector of a Catholic School, and later served as a parish priest. In 1553, he embraced the Lutheran Reformation, and two years later he was named Rector of the Lutheran School at Kolozsvar. In 1557 he was chosen Bishop of the Hungarian section of the Lutheran Churches. The following year he served as spokesman for the Lutheran position, successfully defending his church in public debate with Calvinists. In the long run, though the Calvinists lost the debate, they succeeding in lodging doubts in the mind of the Lutheran Bishop.

In 1559, unable to shake those doubts, Francis David resigned as Lutheran Bishop and cast his lot with the Reformed or Calvinist church. In an effort to end the controversy and contention between the Lutherans and the Calvinists, the King, in keeping with the Edict of Torda (1557) called for a formal disputation between the two in 1561. After the debate it was clear that no grounds for compromising the two positions had been found.

In 1563, The Diet of Torda, reaffirmed and extended the original edict of toleration, ordering "that each may embrace the religion that he prefers without any compulsion, and may be free to support preachers of his own faith, and in the use of the sacraments, and that neither party must do injury or violence to the other."[14] The following year, the King sought one more time to end the controversy between the two branches of the Protestant churches. Giorgio Biandrata, who had been recalled to serve as the King's physician, was charged with organizing a debate between the parties in an effort to clarify and perhaps compose the differences between them. The result of this final effort was an order from the King that the Calvinists and the Lutherans separate into two bodies, each with its own structures of governance. Francis David was chosen as superintendent of the Reformed Churches in Transylvania. As a result of Biandrata's influence with the King, David was also named Court Preacher.

No longer involved in debate with the Lutheran Church for control of the Reformation in Transylvania, the Calvinists now moved on to settle doctrinal questions among themselves. Biandrata, the King's physician, was also pre-eminent among the King's counselors, trusted with diplomatic missions and with religious concerns. Thus, he became a major force in the evolution of the Reformed church in Transylvania. In keeping with the concerns he had explored in Switzerland and in Poland, Biandrata quickly insinuated questions concerning the doctrine of the Trinity into the conversation.

Francis David found this a congenial area for exploration. Indeed, David had read both Servetus and Erasmus. As early as 1560, while he was still a Lutheran, David was questioning the doctrine of the Trinity. Inevitably, he and Biandrata would become natural allies in furthering the Reformation in Transylvania, and leading it in a more radical direction. In 1565, Francis David began addressing doctrinal issues from the pulpit of the great church in Kolozsvar, hoping to clear away both the doctrine of the Trinity and the deity of Jesus before the Calvinists adopted any kind of creedal statement.

Peter Melius, the Superintendent of the Reformed Church in Eastern Hungary began to grow suspicious of David and Biandrata and their intentions. Confirmed in his suspicions by communications from Geneva, Melius began a public attack on the radical reformers. The effect of his attack was to bring the issue of the doctrine of the Trinity and the deity of Jesus to public attention. Ultimately the controversy could not be ignored and a public debate was ordered.

In 1566 a Synod at Gyulafehervar was convened for the purpose of discussing the doctrine of the Trinity and related issues. Once more, Biandrata urged that the only language appropriate for the discussion was the language of scripture, not doctrine or dogma or philosophy, putting his opponents at a severe disadvantage, since discussion of the Trinity emerges only after 325 c.e.. This debate marks the beginning of the Unitarian controversy in Transylvania, and while the debate itself was inconclusive it resulted in the spread of anti-trinitarian views in Hungary and in Transylvania. In an effort to block the spread of heresy, orthodox Calvinists adopted the Helvetic Confession, marking the beginning of an irreparable division between the two wings of the Reformed Church.

While the discussion at Gyulafehervar may have been inconclusive, it clearly did not shake the King's faith in his counselor or his court preacher. He provided the two radical reformers a press with which to publish their teachings to a larger audience. In 1567 they published FALSE AND TRUE KNOWLEDGE OF GOD, a volume which betrays the influence of Servetus. It offered a clear attack upon the doctrine of the Trinity. Using a series of eight pictures drawn from orthodox sources that purported to give visual representation of the doctrine, the book held orthodox teachings up to ridicule. The public was shocked by the treatment of church teaching, and the discussion and debate over the matter increased.

Responding to the growing controversy within the Reformed Church, King John Sigismund scheduled a debate between those defending the Unity of God and Trinitarian ministers. Held in the great hall of the palace, the debate began March 3, 1568, and continued for ten days, starting each day at 5 a.m. Francis David carried the bulk of the argument for the Unitarians and at the conclusion of the debate it was generally conceded that the victory should be awarded to him.

On his return to Kolozsvar, David was greeted by a great throng of the city's citizens. Climbing on a boulder, Francis David preached the gospel of the strict unity of God to the eager crowd. Many of the Saxon residents left Kolozsvar, but the rest of the residents embraced the Unitarian faith as presented by Francis David.

Making good use of the press that had been the gift of the King, Biandrata and David produced a series of books supporting their religious views. Melius and the conservative branch of the Reformed church responded with abuse and slander. In 1569 a debate between Melius and David—this time of six days duration—was held at Varad, a city in that portion of Hungary under the rule of John Sigismund. At the conclusion of the encounter, the King ordered that the Unitarians not be interfered with and decreed: "'Inasmuch as we know that faith is the gift of God and that conscience can't be forced, if one cannot comply with these conditions let him go beyond the Tisza' i.e, leave the country and go to Hungary....'since we demand that in our dominions, there will be freedom of conscience.'"[15]

Though the debate the previous year is often considered the birth of Unitarianism, the debate at Varad in 1569 marked the definitive schism between the Trinitarians and the Unitarians in Transylvania. As if to underscore that fact, Francis David published DE REGNO CHRISTI; DE REGNI ANTICHRISTI, a work which was largely a reprint of Servetus' CHRISTIANISMI RESTITUTIO. In response, Melius redoubled his efforts to counter heresy in Eastern Hungary, but despite his efforts, it began to spread rapidly both there and in Lower Hungary which was under Turkish rule. The Unitarian movement would flourish in Lower Hungary until 1750.

King John Sigismund was now prepared to declare himself religiously. He, his High Chamberlain, Gaspar Bekes, and most of the court become Unitarians in 1569. The majority of the population followed into the new confession. One might question the sincerity of these conversions, wondering if they were more political than religious, were it not for the fact that despite centuries of persecution, the church they created has survived, centering around their ancient rallying cry, " Egy Az Isten," God Is One!

On January 14, 1571, the Diet and the King provided legal recognition to the Unitarian Church, naming Unitarianism, Calvinism, Lutheranism and Catholicism as the four "received" religions of the realm, as distinct from "tolerated" religions. The effect of this act was to provide Unitarians with a degree of security in the face of the changes and challenges that lay ahead. This was John Sigismund's last public act. On the next day, while on a hunting trip, his carriage overturned. King John Sigismund never recovered from his injuries. He died two months later.

By almost any standard, certainly by the standards of his time, King John Sigismund was a remarkable ruler. Following the policy of his mother, he made toleration the hallmark of his reign. When he identified himself as a Unitarian, and found the majority of the nation supporting him, he only demanded of those who disagreed that they live in peace with those with whom they differed. The consequence was that this was one of the few places in Europe where the Reformation was carried out without bloodshed.

John Sigismund died without issue. His will named Gaspar Bekes as his successor. Unfortunately for Bekes, he was out of the country, on a mission for the King, when John Sigismund died. Because his mission was to the Emperor, the Sultan became suspicious and withheld support from Bekes. In Bekes' absence, and in view of the attitude of the Turkish government, the Diet elected Stephen Bathori as King of Transylvania. Bathori, a Maygar and one of the few Catholic magnates left in the country, accepted the throne, making a promise to preserve the liberties of the nation, a promise he kept, although he quickly dismissed most of the Unitarians at court. Giorgio Biandrata was retained as a trusted royal counselor, but Francis David was dismissed as court preacher, the press was confiscated and strict censorship, aimed especially at Unitarian works, was instituted. In 1572, Stephen confirmed the decree defining the four received religions, but he warned that the decree related to those religions as they existed in 1571. He would not tolerate further changes or innovations within the received religions, and any attempt at innovation would be greeted with severe punishment.

Bekes was unwilling to bow to the turn of events which had denied him the throne. Returning to Transylvania, he stirred up an insurrection among the Szeklers, most of whom were Unitarians. In 1575, he was defeated and fled the country. Eventually Bekes would be reconciled to Stephen Bathori, but the Szekler nobles who had followed him into rebellion were severely punished for their support of the pretender, and Unitarianism was further weakened as a consequence.

Stephen Bathori ruled Transylvania directly until 1575. In that year, he was elected King of Poland. Indeed, it was the omnipresent Giorgio Biandrata who negotiated the election with the Polish Diet, successfully defending Stephen against the charge that he was secretly an anti-trinitarian. Stephen retained the crown of Transylvania and appointed his brother, Christopher, as regent. Christopher proved to be more narrow-minded than his brother, but retained Biandrata as a royal counselor.

Despite the hostility and suspicion of the crown, Unitarianism continued to grow in Transylvania during this period, and began to organize itself more formally. In 1576, Francis David was chosen Superintendent or Bishop of the Unitarian churches. However, he was once more reminded that the safety of the Unitarian movement depended upon strict adherence to the standard of faith as it existed in January of 1571 and that no deviation from that standard would be tolerated. At the same time, Stephen sought Catholic missionaries to send into the country. Finding few volunteers, ultimately Stephen would appeal to the Jesuits, who would enter the country in 1579.

Meanwhile, the government began to impose new restrictions on the Unitarians. In 1577, they were forbidden to hold synods anywhere except at Torda or Kolozsvar. The Unitarian Bishop was forbidden to visit the churches, and Unitarians living outside Torda and Kolozsvar were placed under the supervision of the Reformed Bishop who was given the right to attempt their conversion.

Nonetheless, the Unitarians continued to prosper. In 1578, over three hundred ministers participated in the Synod held at Torda. However, Francis David, the Bishop, was not much interested in church organization. His real enthusiasm—as revealed by the history of his passage from Catholicism to Lutheranism to Calvinism to Unitarianism—was for doctrinal reform. The decree that arrested doctrinal development at 1571 was galling, in light of his personal drive for reform of doctrine. He welcomed a decision by the synod that affirmed the right of ministers to discuss and investigate among themselves matters which had not been settled by a general synod.

Almost at once, Francis David began the exploration of such unsettled issues. He concluded that the Lord's Supper is not to be considered a sacrament, but only a meal. It was abandoned at Kolozsvar. Similarly, infant baptism was officially abolished. But most dangerous of all, Francis David began private discussions concerning predestination, and whether it is appropriate to worship Jesus, or invoke him in prayers. When reports of these discussions reached Biandrata, he became deeply alarmed for the future of the Unitarian Church. He immediately wrote to David, warning him not to make a public issue of any of these matters, lest the Prince seize the opportunity to punish the church.

At first, David agreed to avoid public exploration of the matters that were of growing concern for him. However, his personal pondering continued unabated. He continued his private conversations, confiding his deepening convictions in informal ways. At last, as his questions grew into firm convictions, David began to take his doctrinal conclusions into the pulpit of the great church at Kolozsvar.

Thoroughly alarmed, Biandrata tried again to convince David to alter his position. Seeking additional support, he invited Faustus

Socinus to Kolozsvar to dissuade David from his position concerning the adoration of Christ. Socinus was David's house-guest for four months in 1578, but failed to change his host's mind. However, David did agree to submit the issue in writing to the Minor Church of Poland for their consideration and recommendation.

While the reply of the Polish Brethren was pending, Francis David called a synod at Torda. There it was affirmed that "to purify old doctrine from errors and superstition is not innovation; and that a natural consequence of faith in one God is the doctrine that he alone should be worshipped."[16] Armed with the result of the Synod, David began preaching directly to the question, declaring that to invoke Christ is no better than invoking Mary. Biandrata, believing that David had agreed to remain silent until the Poles had replied and then to abide by their decision, felt betrayed by his old colleague.

He responded by bringing pressure to bear on the clergy, threatening them with banishment if they continued to support David. More than this, Biandrata reported David's activities to the Prince, declaring his opposition to David and defining himself as David's enemy. The Prince responded by ordering David to refrain from further preaching. David preached twice on the following Sunday, explaining to the gathered congregations the reasons for his impending arrest.

As he had expected, David was arrested and held for trial before the Diet. At this point the response of the Polish church arrived, supporting Biandrata, as the crafty counselor had known it would. However, the opinion of the Poles was no longer relevant. The question was no longer should Christ be worshipped, but rather was Francis David guilty of innovation.

At the trial, the prosecutor was Giorgio Biandrata. David, ill and weak, defended himself as best he could. He argued that the issue of invoking Christ in prayers was not a new matter, that he and Biandrata and others had opposed it more than eight years before. Biandrata swore that he had never held that view. It became a matter of the word of a rebellious cleric against that of a trusted royal counselor. Many of the nobles supported David; the clergy were split. One Calvinist Hungarian demanded the death penalty; and the Jesuits were eager to see the Unitarian leader condemned. In the end, Francis David was found guilty of innovation and condemned to perpetual imprisonment. He died in the dungeon at Deva, November 15, 1579, a martyr to the cause of Unitarianism in Transylvania, and still the great hero of those who proclaim "God is One!"

In the wake of these events, Biandrata maneuvered a conservative confession of faith for the Unitarian Church, restored infant Baptism and reinstated the Lord's Supper as a commemorative meal. The Prince named Demetrius Hunyadi as David's successor as Unitarian Bishop. After 1580, Biandrata's influence in the church waned. He died in 1588, little mourned by the religious movement he had done so very much to create.

The great tragedy of David and Biandrata lies in the fact that each of them was committed to the salvation of the Unitarian cause. Biandrata acted to save the church from political peril. In a letter to Jacobus Palaeologus written in 1580, Biandrata suggested that he was less disturbed by David's ideas than by their possible consequences for the future of the church. David wanted to advance needed reform, even at the expense of constant and recurring conflict. This, he seemed to believe, was the mission of the church, and he was prepared to risk everything, his own well-being and the well-being of the church, in the pursuit of greater truth and purity of doctrine.

In the years that followed the deaths of the two great instigators, the Unitarian Church in Transylvania avoided the tragedy which ended the history of the Minor Church of Poland. Its existence protected by its status as one of the four received religions, it survived within the context of the decree which tied it to the faith and the creed of 1571 and forced it into apparent doctrinal stagnation for over two centuries.

Hunyadi, David's successor as Bishop, proved to be an able administrator. During his tenure, he called annual synods of the church, organized the church into twelve districts, each with a dean, organized education for the children, and on occasion engaged in debates with the Jesuits who worked to introduce a revitalized Catholicism into Transylvania. When Hunyadi died in 1592, he left a church which was well organized and on safe-ground. While it appeared to conform to the standard of 1571, many of the ministers continued private support of the opinions and beliefs that had lead Francis David to martyrdom. In 1597, at the time of the death of Hunyadi's successor, George Enyedi the Unitarians counted more than four hundred churches. In the turmoil of the years to come Transylvanian Unitarians would have cause to be grateful for the organizational skills of Hunyadi and Enyedi.

In 1581, Prince Christopher Bathori, who had succeeded his brother Stephen, died and was succeeded by Sigismund Bathori who had been schooled by Jesuits and who was heavily influenced by Austria. In 1595, his underlying sympathy for Austria led Sigismund to make Transylvania a fiefdom of Emperor Rudolf of Austria, thus abrogating the treaty with Turkey that had guaranteed Transylvanian independence. Those who opposed the alliance with Austria were executed, among them five leading Unitarians.

In 1597, a protracted struggle for the throne began when Sigismund abdicated the throne in favor of Rudolf of Austria, then changed his mind, then abdicated again, this time in favor of his cousin, Cardinal Andrew Bathori. Rudolf, determined to exert his claim to the territory, dispatched an army under the command of George Basta to secure his rights.

The result was a six-year reign of terror in Transylvania, with the brunt of the terror falling on Protestants and doubly on Unitarian Protestants. Churches were seized and transferred to the Catholics; Unitarians were forced to embrace Catholicism on pain of death.

In 1599 Andrew Bathori was killed in battle and succeeded by the Wallachian Count Michael, who also ravaged the countryside. The following year Sigismund returned and routed Michael. Michael and Basta then combined their forces to defeat Sigismund.

In 1602 a Unitarian, Mozes Szekeley raised the standard of revolt. With the aid of the Sultan, he succeeded in driving Michael and Basta out of Transylvania and was proclaimed Prince in 1603. Basta and Michael returned with new forces and Mozes Szekeley was killed in battle. In retaliation for the rebellion, Basta ravaged the country anew. He decreed that only Catholic worship would be permitted in the "disloyal cities." The great church at Kolozsvar was given to the Jesuits. Laboring under special persecution, the Unitarians were forced to meet in secret for three years. In 1605 Stephen Bocskai raised a new revolt and succeeded in being crowned Prince of Transylvania and Hungary in 1605. Bocskai, a staunch Calvinist, nevertheless respected the tradition of tolerance. He proclaimed religious liberty and restored churches to the Unitarians. Bocskai had ruled for only six months when he suddenly died, a victim of poison it was rumored. His successor, Gabriel Bathori, another committed Calvinist, took the oath to respect the religious traditions of the realm and immediately set about to repress Catholics and Unitarians alike. In turn, his successor, Gabriel Bethlen extended religious freedom to Catholics and Lutherans but repressed the Unitarians. In this period, over one hundred Unitarian ministers were driven from their pulpits, and replaced with Calvinists.

During this time of intense public turmoil, the internal life of the Unitarian Church continued to evolve. Although innovation was forbidden, changes were privately adopted by ministers and churches and those changes influenced the public expression of Unitarianism. Among those changes was a move to regard the Old Testament as normative, particularly those injunctions which required believers to abstain from pork and from blood, and to observe the sabbath. By 1600, the more radical Judaizers or

Sabbatarians, though mostly Unitarian in origin, were virtually a separate religion. When authorities determined to suppress the Sabbatarians in the period between 1618 and 1638, the policy of repression offered an opportunity to include Unitarians in that repression. In 1618, the Unitarian Synod was presided over by a Calvinist Bishop. In 1622 some sixty-two churches were seized and converted to Calvinist use.

In 1638 the Diet of Dees decreed a new creed for Unitarians, which called for worship of Christ, but not as God, re-institution of infant baptisms, which had been allowed to lapse, and the observance of the Lord's supper. At the same time, the church was forbidden to publish and was warned that innovation would be punished by the state. The decree had the effect of limiting the freedom of belief of the Unitarian Church, but securing the continued existence of the church within the definition offered by the decree. The Agreement of Dees remained the official standard of the Unitarian Church in Transylvania into the twentieth century. It has sometimes been changed by interpretation, but never by amendment.

This does not mean that the church would face no more trials. As the Turkish threat to Europe receded and Transylvania became part of the Austro-Hungarian Empire, its fortunes fluctuated with the attitudes of the rulers. Under Leopold I (1657-1705) churches, schools, and endowments were confiscated, but Unitarian Bishops were permitted to supervise the Szekler churches and a press was permitted.

Joseph I (1705-1711) observed toleration, but his successor, Charles III (1711-1740) allowed Unitarian Churches to be despoiled for two generations. Indeed, in 1728 there was an attempt to outlaw Unitarianism completely, an effort frustrated by the fact that Protestants of all labels, sensing a common threat, united in opposition. Under Maria Theresa (1740-1780) the government created a fund for the conversion of Unitarian children, decreed that no non-Unitarian might marry a Unitarian, prohibited any public discussion of

Unitarianism, forbade conversions to Unitarianism, closed Unitarian schools, and refused to permit any new churches to be built or any existing churches to be repaired.

By the time of Maria Theresa's death there were 125 churches with some 50,00 members remaining, and the Unitarians were sustaining a school and a college. Her successors took the oath of toleration more seriously, abolished censorship, and allowed the church more latitude. However, the revolution of 1848, and wars between Russia and Austria brought a renewed threat of repression. Only financial intervention by English Unitarians, who had recently discovered their Eastern European cousins, saved the Transylvanian schools affiliated with the Unitarian Church. The First and Second World Wars brought new devastation to the country and particularly to the Unitarian portion of the population. The period of Cold War Communism inflicted severe limitations upon the life of the Unitarian churches of Transylvania, with ministers being imprisoned and Unitarian villages threatened with destruction. And yet the fact remains that despite centuries of repression, the Unitarian Church still survives in the land where it was first called by that name and still seeks to fulfill its ancient commitment to reason and tolerance and the ancient cry that "God Is One!

HOLLAND AND ENGLAND

There was never an indigenous Unitarian or Universalist movement in Holland, but the political, geographical and religious situation of the Low Countries combined to make that region of Western Europe the vector through which the thought of Polish Socinians and Transylvanian Unitarians would be introduced into England. In order to better understand the roots of Unitarianism in England, it is well that we briefly visit the history of liberal religion in Holland.

Geographically, the Netherlands was a major crossroad for all of Europe. The terminus for all commerce moving down the Rhine, it was a major focus of the Mediterranean trade. It was a center for the movement of trade and people travelling to and from the Baltic, Scandinavia and Eastern Europe. It was England's major trading partner. Inevitably, all the ideas, concerns, issues and enthusiasms which flitted across Europe moved with trade and travelers to Holland, whence it was exported to other lands.

During the sixteenth century, the Spanish Hapsburgs, the most Catholic ruling house in Europe, governed the Low Countries. What is more, the Netherlands and Spain were both ruled directly by Charles V, who, as the Holy Roman Emperor, had to deal with Luther and the Protestant rebellion in his German possessions. Charles had been raised in Holland and always had a special affinity for the region. He retained the affection of the majority of the population during his reign but even the special relationship that existed between the Emperor and his Dutch citizens was not adequate to keep the Netherlands free of the contagion of Reformation thought. Lutheran reforms made their way across the Rhine almost at once. Anabaptists, from their bases in Switzerland and along the Rhine, invaded the Netherlands on the heels of the Lutherans. Calvinism entered the Netherlands in due course.

In 1535, after the Munster rebellion had been crushed and the German Peasant's rebellion had been beaten down, authorities in the Netherlands began a major repression of the Anabaptists within their boundaries. Thousands of these religious radicals were driven from their homes, many of them killed. The tattered remnants, rallied by Menno Simons and purged of their radicalism, withdrew from the world and became an inward-looking sect known as Mennonites. Catholics retained control of the Netherlands until the end of the reign of Charles V, though Lutherans and Calvinists continued to grow and press for reform.

In 1555, Charles abdicated in favor of his son, Phillip II. Unlike his father, Phillip had little knowledge of or interest in the Netherlands. He increased taxes, appointed Spanish officials to govern the provinces, quartered troops on the people, introduced the Inquisition, and subordinated the interests of the Netherlands to those of Spain. In the process he alienated the people who had been such staunch supporters of his father. Protestants succeeded in identifying their hopes for religious reform with the growing national demand for independence, a combination that Phillip would find impossible to defeat.

For a while, Phillip held his own in dealing with a nation which included—in addition to Catholics—Lutherans, Calvinists and Anabaptists. The Protestants, divided against each other, found it difficult to present a united front. It was not uncommon to find one Protestant group joining the Catholic party to frustrate another Protestant group. However, as resistance to Phillip grew, the opposition gradually came to be dominated by Calvinists and was consolidated under their leadership.

The man who was able to unite the fragmented Protestants and nationalists into a formidable force was William of Orange. A favorite of Charles V, William had been alienated by his discovery of the existence of a secret treaty between France and Spain which called for the two nations to unite to extirpate heresy in their own territories and in the Netherlands. William, a strong nationalist, was further alienated by the rule of Phillip II and his callous attitude toward his Dutch subjects. Increasingly, William's thoughts turned to rebellion. In Calvinism, with its doctrinal notion that lower officials have an obligation to defend the liberties of the people even against higher authorities, William found a religious justification for his struggle. He knew, however, that a successful rebellion would require foreign support.

William sought the aid of the Lutheran powers of Germany. They were unwilling to provide the aid he sought unless the Calvinists in Holland were prepared to embrace Lutheranism—a condition William knew he could not meet. He then turned in the other direction, toward England. Elizabeth I, already on bad terms with Spain and

Phillip II, was prepared to offer modest support.

His next step was to attempt to unite his fragmented and fractious people. He proposed, for example, that each city might be divided into five ghettos, one for each of the Christian sects and a separate one for Jews. The proposal was never put into practice. William worked assiduously to find a mechanism to promote religious tolerance, convinced that sectarian conflict would defeat his efforts to drive out the Spanish. In 1578 in the Peace of Antwerp it was agreed that each should be free in the practice of religion since each would ultimately have to answer to God. The arrangement was short lived as a consequence of intolerance on all sides.

Ultimately, the Spaniards lost control of their possessions in the Lowlands, and the Netherlands split on religious lines. Belgium would remain Catholic, conservative and dominated by the nobility and the clergy. Holland would become Protestant, largely Calvinist. In 1581 the Dutch Republic was declared. Some exchange of population occurred between the two regions, and as a result, Holland became rigorously Calvinist. However, the legacy of William of Orange and the geographical and political realities worked to moderate that Calvinism over time. Penalties for dissenting thought became less extreme, and repressive laws which had not been moderated were largely ignored, eventually making Holland the most tolerant nation in Western Europe, and a place of refuge for peoples driven from their homes for religious reasons.

The most frequent route of travel from Eastern to Western Europe during the sixteenth century was by ship from Danzig to Amsterdam. Polish students travelling to Universities in Western Europe, found that their journey took them through Holland. Clergy, many of whom brought with them books from the Socinian Press, usually accompanied such students. In 1598, Christoff Ostorodt and Andrew Wojdowski visited Amsterdam and Leiden on one such journey. Their books were seized by the authorities, and when the nature of the contents had been discovered, the two Poles were ordered out of the country. The confiscated books were condemned as heretical and ordered burned. However, before the order could be carried out, the offending volumes disappeared. One wonders how often these and other banned books were circulated secretly and read by inquisitive readers.

In any case, early in the seventeenth century doctrinal ferment erupted in the Dutch Reformed Church, providing Socinians an opportunity to extend their gospel. Most susceptible to Socinian influence was the liberal wing of the Reformed church, those called Remonstrants because they had remonstrated against strict Calvinist views. Led by Jacob Arminius, (from whom Arminianism derived its name) the Remonstrants rejected strict predestinarianism and insisted that individuals could influence their own salvation. Central to the Remonstrants' position was a strong demand for religious tolerance. They were accused by their opponents of Socinian errors. Indeed, they did publish some Socinian works. In addition, in 1614 Servetus' ERRORS OF THE TRINITY was translated and published in Holland.

Whatever agreements the Remonstrants may have had with Socinianism, they also had some areas of disagreement. Nonetheless, when the Synod of Dort exiled the religious liberals in 1619, accusing them of political liberalism, Polish Socinians expressed deep concern for their plight and invited them to Poland. A number of the exiles accepted the invitation and sought refuge among the Polish Socinians. In time, most of the exiles would gradually filter back to their homes in Holland, bringing with them a deeper understanding and appreciation of Socinian thought and practice.

In 1630, the former exiles were granted freedom of residence and the right to build schools and churches in Holland. Three years later the Remonstrants founded a seminary. However, their experience had made of them a separate people. They rebuffed the efforts of Martin Ruar to unite all Calvinists, thus confirming the conservative's conviction that the Remonstrants represented a growing heresy, as Socinian ideas spread throughout Holland.

In response, a number of decrees against the liberals were passed, but they were only sporadically enforced. On occasion some books would be burned. Sometimes fines would be levied. In truth, however, there was little stomach for strict enforcement and consequently Socinian ideas continued to influence the religious thought of the Dutch people. Indeed, the influence of Socinianism was not confined to the Remonstrants, but emerged also within the Mennonite movement.

Evidence of this Socinian influence can be seen in the Collegiant movement. This lay-led movement emerged at first among the Remonstrants, and later became independent of them. Broad tolerance was a primary principle among the Collegiants, allowing for discussion of religious beliefs ranging from Calvinism to Socinianism to Judaism, and including within its embrace the great philosopher, Spinoza.

In 1665, the Racovian Catechism was republished in Holland. In 1668, the BIBLIOTHECA FRATRUM POLONORUM, the Library of the Polish Brethren, was published in Holland, making available to Western Europe the central documents of the Socinian Reformers. It is not surprising that many of the Polish refugees who fled their homes when the Minor Church of Poland was forced out of existence sought and found succor in Holland. There was never a single forceful leader among the Socinians in Holland, nor were there ever separate Socinian Churches. Socinians and their ideas were received by Mennonites, Remonstrants and Collegiants alike and through them leavened and liberalized Protestant thought in Holland, making it the most liberal and tolerant of the Western European nations. It was from Holland that Socinianism would enter England and influence the emergence of English Unitarianism.

England had always been restive under the rule of the Roman Church. Early on, Celtic traditions of a Christianity centered upon abbots and monasteries had clashed with Roman traditions centered upon bishops and parishes. Theologically, Britain and Rome clashed over the teachings of Pelagius who had taught that human beings have the power to influence their own salvation. Henry II and Thomas Becket had played out the tragic conflict between church and state, and resentment over the role of the church and its financial demands could be encountered at almost any point in English History.

Well before the Reformation, doctrinal heterodoxy occasionally emerged among the inhabitants of the British Isles. In 1327, one Adam Duff O'Toole was burned in Dublin for denying the Trinity. In 1401, William Sawtrey of Lynn was burned for the same offense. These latent tendencies toward heterodoxy were aided and abetted in the late fourteenth century when John Wycliff translated the Bible into English so that common people might read sacred writ and judge its meaning for themselves. His followers, the Lollards, burst the bonds of the church's doctrinal system and strayed into various heresies, anti-trinitarianism among them.

Despite this background, the English Reformation emerged, almost by accident and as a by-product of the complex domestic and political situation confronting England at the end of the fifteenth and the beginning of the sixteenth century. For decades the Island Kingdom had been torn apart by the Wars of the Roses, in which the House of York and the House of Lancaster battled each other for the throne. The Civil struggle ended when Henry Tudor defeated Richard III and assumed the throne as Henry VII. Henry, of the house of Lancaster, married Elizabeth of York, thus uniting the two warring houses. However, feeling insecure on his throne, and seeking a foreign alliance that would lend legitimacy and stability to his new dynasty, Henry arranged a marriage between his son, Arthur and Catherine of Aragon, daughter of Ferdinand and Isabella of Spain. The marriage brought Henry an alliance with the strongest power on the continent, and a substantial dowry to fatten the treasury of the miserly monarch.

Immediately after the marriage, Arthur died, leaving Catherine a widow, and leaving both the alliance and the dowry in question. Unwilling to lose either, Henry moved to secure both by proposing that Catherine be married to his second son, Henry. Unfortunately, under church law, Henry and Catherine were unable to wed, since Catherine's first marriage established a relationship with Henry that barred marriage between the two of them. Henry VII, as was customary at the time, approached the Pope for a dispensation that would permit the marriage; the Pope, as was customary at the time, granted the dispensation; and in due course, Henry and Catherine were married. Upon the death of his father, Henry assumed the throne of England as Henry VIII.

Henry VIII prided himself on his skill as an accomplished athlete, warrior, and dancer and his mastery of arts and knowledge. Educated in the style of the new humanism, he was a poet, a musician, a master of languages, and a theologian of sorts. He did not hesitate to write a response to Luther, which so pleased the Pope that he named Henry, Defender of the Faith—a title which British Monarchs flaunt to this day. Unfortunately for Henry and Catherine, they failed to accomplish the one task necessary for a new dynasty— that they produce a viable heir to the throne. Henry fathered an illegitimate son, but despite a number of pregnancies, Catherine's only surviving child was a daughter, Mary.

In time, Henry became convinced that the failure to produce an heir was occasioned by the fact that the marriage between the royal pair, the papal dispensation notwithstanding, was contrary to God's law. Henry sought to have the marriage annulled, a request which he expected to be granted and which, under normal circumstances, would have been granted. However, these were not normal times; the Pope was under threat from two directions at once. The Reformation's attack on the authority of Rome made it inconvenient to declare the dispensation of a previous Pope erroneous. What is more, Catherine, Henry's wife, was the Aunt of Charles V, King of

Spain and Holy Roman Emperor, whose troops were poised in Northern Italy, and who could be expected to react with political and personal anger at a decision which determined that Catherine was living in sin, and that Mary was a bastard. And so, the Pope delayed and temporized, and played for time, while Henry became more and more impatient to rid himself of Catherine, acquire a new queen and produce the heir who would be a guarantee against the renewal of civil war upon Henry's death.

In 1534, unwilling to wait any longer, Henry maneuvered Parliament into declaring him "Head of the Church in England." The purpose of this action was not to change doctrine or practice in the English church, but to make it independent of Rome, dependent upon the King, and therefore a pliant tool in the quest for an annulment of the King's inconvenient and unproductive marriage. The effect of the act, however, was to throw England into the arms of the Protestant Reformation. Needing allies on the Continent, and unable to find allies among the Catholic powers, Henry, of necessity, sought those allies among the Protestant states. In turn, unwilling to antagonize his continental allies, Henry had little choice but to welcome Protestant refugees to England, making the Island Kingdom a haven for those driven from their homes.

In 1535, on the heels of the debacle at Munster, and in the wake of the persecutions in the Netherlands, many Anabaptist refugees fled to England seeking a modicum of safety. Inevitably, among these refugees were a number of Arians and anti-trinitarians. Henry, like most non-Catholic rulers, did not feel that the safety of his realm demanded that he tolerate radical reform. The Anabaptists in England were persecuted and harassed. Indeed, during Henry's reign, twenty-six were burned for heresy, fourteen for denying the trinity. But despite the repression, the Anabaptists continued to grow in number.

Henry's second marriage produced only another daughter, christened Elizabeth. His third marriage was more successful, producing the heir for which he and all England had waited, a son christened Edward. Despite three more marriages, Henry produced no more heirs.

When Henry died in 1547, his son, who assumed the throne as Edward VI, was still a child. The affairs of state were entrusted to a Privy Council whose members, with the Support of the Archbishop of Canterbury, Thomas Cranmer, were far more committed than Henry had been to a thorough reform of the English church. Their hope was to reform and redefine the doctrine of the church, while building a barrier against the more radical Anabaptist, antitrinitarian views. Cranmer invited European scholars to England with the view in mind of strengthening the Reformation of the English Church. Among those who responded to this invitation were Bernardo Ochino and Laelius Socinus.

So many other, less well-known foreigners were attracted by England's friendly welcome that more than three thousand religious refugees of one type or another flooded London. In 1550, a congregation known as The Church of the Strangers was established in London, charged with serving the religious needs of foreign Protestants. The first superintendent of the Church of the Strangers was Jan Laski, a Pole whom we met in the story of the emergence of the Socinian movement in Poland. Inevitably, the Church of the Strangers became a center for the expression and the spread of a variety of unorthodox views. Particularly troublesome was the spread of Arianism within this body. Indeed, in 1551, one member of the Church, Dr. George Van Parris, was burned for his insistence that only God is God.

Edward VI, his health always precarious, died in 1553, before reaching his majority. His successor was his half-sister, Mary, daughter of Catherine of Aragon. Mary was a devout Catholic by personal conviction and by political necessity. The Catholic Church had never wavered in its insistence that the marriage between Henry and Catherine was legal and binding. It had been the Protestants who agreed that the marriage had never been legal and that Mary was a bastard. Her deep, personal Catholic faith was also essential to her claim to the throne.

Mary, unlike her contemporary, Isabella of Transylvania, was not content to be the Catholic ruler of a Protestant kingdom. She set about to reverse the political and religious developments of Edward's brief reign. She allied her kingdom with the Catholic powers of Europe, especially the Spain of Phillip II, whom she married. She acted to remove Protestants from positions of influence in the state and the church. Immediately the Church of the Strangers was disbanded. Some three hundred Protestants were put to death for their convictions, earning the Queen the enduring nickname, "Bloody Mary." And, of course the flow of refugees was reversed as Protestants fled England, seeking refuge in Europe.

Mary's brief reign ended with her death in 1558. She was followed on the throne by the greatest of the Tudor monarchs, Elizabeth I. If Mary had to be Catholic, Elizabeth had no choice but to be Protestant. In the eyes of the Roman Church, she was the illegitimate child of a bigamous and illicit union. It was Protestantism which had sanctified the marriage of her parents and which now regarded her not only as the legitimate monarch, but their great hope for the future. Elizabeth would seek allies among the Protestants, especially the Dutch and all her life she would remain suspicious of Catholic plots to depose her.

Like her father, Elizabeth was not eager to embrace a radical form of Protestantism. Indeed, her effort was to create a compromise between Luther and Calvin in doctrine and between Catholic and Protestant in worship and ceremony. Compromises, by their very nature, rarely satisfy anyone, but Elizabeth's dream faced an especially difficult challenge. With her accession to the throne, Protestant exiles began to return home from Europe, bringing with them a new radicalism acquired during their years on the Continent. Many of them came home committed to a purified English church, not a compromise. It is in this development that the roots of Puritanism are to be found.

In 1559, Elizabeth permitted the re-establishment of the Church of the Strangers. She abolished laws for burning heretics, but in the Act of Uniformity required everyone to worship either in the Church of England or the Church of the Strangers. Finding neither alternative acceptable, many Anabaptists chose to meet for worship separately and in secret. As this practice became known, it resulted in an order banishing Anabaptists from England in 1560, and the persecution of those who failed to leave.

In response to this persecution, Jacobus Acontius wrote a plea for tolerance, suggesting that only the language of the scriptures should be used in doctrinal discussions. He argued that by the standard of the scriptures, doctrines such as the Trinity, the Deity of Christ, the meaning of the Lord's Supper are not essential and therefore should not be insisted upon, nor should people be persecuted because of disagreement about such lightly supported and dubious doctrines.

Acontius' reasoning sounds familiar—the same logic which religious radicals and liberals had urged in Poland, Transylvania, Holland and elsewhere. It had little effect on official policy in England. Anabaptists continued to grow and spread their teachings all the while the government continued to persecute them. In 1575 Elizabeth revived the laws for the burning of heretics. Among those who suffered under this renewal of persecution were a number of people whose heresy involved unorthodox views of the incarnation and the Trinity. The County of Norfolk was a center of such opinions. Here, heterodox views of the Trinity were rife among the common people. And here it was that wheelwrights and tanners, goldsmiths and plow-wrights were burned for their refusal to accept traditional teachings about the Triune God.

For all her long reign, Elizabeth sought to create a national church which was broadly inclusive and which blended Protestant and

Catholic practice. However, the Elizabethan compromise did not include those who questioned the deity of Jesus or the Doctrine of the Trinity. And of necessity, it could not include those who believed with all their beings that the church must be purged, cleansed and purified of every vestige of Roman Catholicism. When Elizabeth died in 1603, these conflicts within the Church of England would remain to confront her successor, James I, and plague the Stuart rulers who would follow him.

On his accession to the throne, James I of England and IV of Scotland, seeking unity within the boundaries of his new kingdom, outlawed all religious gatherings outside the Church of England. The immediate effect of this edict was the imprisonment of those who refused to abide by its dictate and an occasional execution of the more recalcitrant. (The last burning for heresy would occur in 1612.) The long-term effect was to force into the open the latent struggle over the structure of the Church of England.

In a curious way, this controversy by-passed the heretical sects and their challenge to traditional doctrine. It focused, instead, upon the government of the church and its liturgical forms. Henry VIII had envisioned a church which was Catholic in every way but one— he and not the Pope would be its head on earth. Elizabeth's compromise had centered on a similar model, with authority flowing from monarch and parliament through archbishops and bishops. The Protestants who had returned to England after Mary's death had brought with them a dream of a more thoroughly reformed church, a church purified of all traces of Catholicism. They were convinced that this purified church could not be achieved unless the structure of governance, the polity of the church was changed. They sought a presbyterian polity that would remove power from bishops and place it in the hands of presbyteries, thus making reform from below possible. The conflict that resulted demanded the attention of the English church through most of the seventeenth century.

This conflict would eventually involve government and parliament, provoke a civil war and cost one Stuart king his head. While all of England was caught up in this struggle, Socinian influences were quietly penetrating the country. When the Racovian Catechism, dedicated to James I, appeared in England in 1614, it was publicly burned. But the books from the press at Rakow and translations of those books from Holland continued to enter the country, to be read secretly and discussed privately. Their influence was reinforced on occasion when Polish scholars and nobles visited England on their trips to the west.

In the mid-century a movement appeared within the Church of England which, while not Socinian, clearly reflected the Socinian concern for tolerance. The Latitudinarian Movement sought to end conflict within the church by proposing a national church which would be as broadly inclusive as possible. This church would insist upon the smallest number of doctrines possible. Leaders of the group included Lucius Cary (Lord Falkland), John Hales of Eton, and William Chillingworth. They argued that the Bible and the open mind are the standards of faith, that only doctrines plainly taught in the Bible are essential, and those are both few in number and obvious, all other doctrines being arbitrary and unnecessary. It is small wonder that the Latitudinarians were accused of being Socinians. The effect of their movement would be that it created an atmosphere within the Church of England which, when the time was right, would permit Unitarianism a hearing.

In truth, this concern for latitude in doctrine was a consequence of the on-going struggle over the government of the church. Increasingly, the Episcopal party was concerned more for unity of form than for unity of doctrine. Their opponents saw amendment of polity as a vehicle for strict purification of doctrine. So long as the Presbyterians and the Episcopalians struggled with each other for control of the Church of England, Socinianism could grow quietly within the church as well as outside it.

The first Presbytery in England had been formed in 1572 and began to worship apart from the Church of England. For two generations it grew and spread, largely among the middle class, despite sporadic attempts to outlaw any alternative to the Church of England. By 1640 the Presbyterian party had gained ascendancy in parliament and found itself confronting King Charles in a struggle which would pit the Presbyterians or Puritans against the Church of England, and parliament against monarch. It was in that year that a convocation of Presbyterians called for political measures to stop the spread of the damnable and cursed heresy of Socinianism. Books were ordered banned and preaching of Socinianism was forbidden. Such measures went unenforced when parliament concluded that the convocation had exceeded its authority.

In 1643, parliament, dominated by Presbyterians, called a meeting to settle the government and the liturgy of the Church of England. One hundred twenty-one clergymen attended, along with thirty laymen as advisors. Finding themselves outnumbered, the Episcopalians withdrew. The remaining group approved a confession of faith, called The Westminster Confession, prepared a catechism, a directory of worship to replace the Book of Common Prayer, and a plan for government of the church by presbyteries rather than by bishops. The plan was never fully implemented except in London and Lancashire. The Episcopalians refused to accept it and joined a group of dissidents, known as Independents who insisted upon tolerance, to thwart implementation of the plan. The Puritans charged, in response, that Socinianism was eating away at the church and urged that Christians have no communion with any who deny the Trinity.

In 1645, a Member of Parliament, Paul Best, was charged before the House of Commons with denying the Trinity and the deity of Christ. Best had traveled to Germany, Poland and to Transylvania and in the process had become a Unitarian. The House of Commons found him guilty of heresy and condemned him to be hanged. Eventually, however, he was released.

In 1648, Parliament passed an Act for Punishing Blasphemies and Heresy, the so-called "Draconian Ordinance," the final fruit of long years of Presbyterian efforts to use law to enforce theological conformity. Under the terms of this act, the death penalty was to be imposed on anyone convicted of denying the Trinity. The ordinances were never enforced, primarily because the Independents were the rising power in Parliament, and their insistence on tolerance served to make of it a dead letter.

It is against this background that Unitarianism emerged in England. The movement has at least four sources, including the heretical explorations that emerged as a consequence of the translation of the Bible into English by Wycliff, Tyndale, et al.; the influence of the Church of the Strangers with its 5,000 members and branches in eleven towns bringing the influence of Italian Humanists to the Island Kingdom; the influx of Anabaptists after 1535; and Socinian books and tracts urging reason in religion, tolerance of diversity, and use of scripture as source of religious language. These influences would emerge in a variety of ways in the various competing religious alternatives that English Protestantism offered. Thus, Presbyterians, Independents, Separatists, Dissenters, and Episcopalians all contributed to the emergence of British Unitarianism.

At this point the story comes to focus upon the man who has been called "the father of English Unitarianism." John Biddle, born in 1615, was the son of a tailor or woolen draper. At nineteen, John was a student at Oxford; subsequently he became a tutor, and in 1641 received his M.A. Biddle was a biblicist who knew the New Testament by heart both in English and in Greek. However, he was described as a man "determined more by reason than authority."[17] Through his own study of scripture he came to the conclusion that the Doctrine of the Trinity had no support in scripture, nor could it be rescued by an appeal to reason.

In 1644, Biddle shared his convictions with others and immediately was called before a magistrate to defend himself against a charge of heresy. In response he submitted a confession of faith, which the court found less than satisfactory. Biddle rewrote the confession of faith to the satisfaction of the court and was released from custody.

The court freed Biddle but he felt growing discomfort with the statement, which had obtained his release. He began writing a work entitled TWELVE ARGUMENTS DRAWN OUT OF SCRIPTURE, in which he set about to refute the Doctrine of the Trinity, using the New Testament as his authority. Biddle was betrayed to the magistrate by a friend and immediately jailed. He was held for trial before Parliament, but was bailed out by a friend in Gloucester. Six months later, Biddle was summoned to London. Once there, he found his trial had been postponed. He appealed to the authorities for a speedy trial, but to no effect. He was held under house arrest for five years. Biddle used his time to put his TWELVE ARGUMENTS through the press. When released, it aroused a great deal of controversy and was burned by the public hangman. Nonetheless, a second edition was printed before the end of the year.

Encouraged by the response, Biddle completed work on two additional tracts. CONFESSIONS OF FAITH TOUCHING THE HOLY TRINITY ACCORDING TO THE SCRIPTURE argued that Christ has only a human nature, but is the Son of God as a consequence of God's act—a position very close to that of Servetus. THE TESTIMONIES CONCERNING THAT ONE GOD AND THE PERSONS OF THE HOLY TRINITY examined the works of six early church fathers and six later writers to support Biddle's views. These tracts engendered a number of responses, to which Biddle, with ample time on his hands, was able to reply.

After the execution of Charles I (1649), Oliver Cromwell, who drew much of his political support from the Independents, leaned toward tolerance in religious matters. Biddle's confinement was eased. A friend was allowed to post bail for him, and Biddle was permitted to move to Staffordshire, where he became chaplain to the Justice of the Peace and preacher at a neighboring church. When news of this development reached London, the presiding judge in his case recalled him to confinement. Back in prison, Biddle used his time correcting proofs for a new edition of the Septuagint

In 1652, Cromwell issued the Act of Oblivion, a general amnesty setting free all those accused of crime. John Biddle was among those released. Immediately he gathered a congregation for Sunday worship and the study of the scriptures. He and his followers came to be known as Biddellians or Socinians. When the existence of this congregation came to light, the London clergy were thoroughly alarmed, but by this time there was no law to use against Biddle and his followers, even though, in the same year, a reprint of the Racovian Catechism was ordered burned.

In 1653, Cromwell became Protector of the Commonwealth and in his oath of office promised freedom of religion to all professing Christians. The following year, Biddle published again, a catechism in which he ignored controverted dogmas, asked scripture-based questions, and defined Christianity in simple, scriptural language. As a consequence, although he discussed God in very anthropomorphic terms he rejected the Doctrine of the Trinity and the Deity of Jesus. The reaction to this work was strong and hostile. Biddle's work was compared to the Racovian Catechism.

Biddle was jailed and called to trial before Parliament. His book was seized and burned. In December, Biddle was sentenced to prison. In May he was freed. Immediately he gathered his followers, by this time increased in numbers, and resumed his ministry among them. Shortly thereafter, Biddle agreed to debate the Deity of Christ with a Baptist preacher. When word of the impending debate reached the authorities, Biddle was arrested and imprisoned again.

Cromwell now found himself pressured from both sides to deal with Biddle's case. He took the matter into his own hands and banished Biddle to the Scilly Isles. Even this did not end the matter, for

Biddle's followers began a ceaseless agitation for his release, an effort that eventually proved successful. Biddle was released and began meeting with his followers again.

In 1660, Charles II was recalled to the throne. Immediately, Charles issued a ban on all non-conformist worship. Biddle, having learned a bit of caution over the years, began to hold his meetings in private. Eventually, of course, this subterfuge was discovered and John Biddle was hauled off to prison and fined one hundred pounds. Unable to pay the fine, he remained in jail. This time, while in confinement, Biddle fell ill. He died in September 1662, two days after his release, a victim of the disease he had contracted while a prisoner.

Despite all his written discourses concerning the Doctrine of the Trinity and the Deity of Jesus, Biddle's real concern had been for a moral and holy life. He is quoted as saying, "No religion would benefit a bad man."[18] Perhaps it was this concern for piety that explains the obvious hold he had over his faithful followers. It may also explain why, with Biddle removed from the scene, his followers soon dispersed, leaving no permanent institutional legacy.

When Oliver Cromwell died in 1660 and Charles II was called to the throne, the Presbyterian, Puritan party looked to this event with great hope. Cromwell and the Independents had thwarted the dream of a purified church governed by presbyteries. Perhaps the new monarch would be more sympathetic and support their dreams in exchange for their support of his rule. Almost immediately, Charles disappointed them, when he declared that Presbyterianism is "no religion for a gentleman."[19]

A Catholic at heart, Charles II sided with the Episcopalian party, and sought to establish religious peace in his realm by enforcing uniformity of worship throughout the kingdom. In 1661, Parliament passed the Corporation Act, which excluded all non-Anglicans from holding municipal office. A year later, the Act of Uniformity required that all clergy declare their full acceptance of the Book of Common

Prayer. It further ordered that clergy not ordained Episcopally would no longer be permitted to preach. Puritan clergy were given three months to meet the demands of this act. In the end 2,257 Puritan clergy were ejected from their offices for failure to conform.[20] They, and the congregations that supported them would be known as Protestant Nonconformists. In time some of the Nonconformists congregations would drift into Unitarianism.

It should be noted that Charles' policy once more focused on questions of forms of worship—free versus liturgical worship, prescribed or voluntary prayer, the garb worn by the clergy, the elements in the services of worship—while ignoring questions of doctrine. As the struggle over outward forms dominated public attention, heretical doctrines continued to develop. Socinian and Arian books were being written and circulated and their influence could be seen in a variety of ways. In this period, the Quakers came into being. Among the Quakers, the earliest systematic works published around 1676 simply ignored the Doctrine of the Trinity. William Penn, the great Quaker leader, and follower of George Fox, denied the Doctrine of the Trinity in 1668 and was briefly jailed for that reason. The Puritan poet, John Milton, completed a theological work, ON CHRISTIAN DOCTRINE, which he instructed should be published after his death. When Milton died in 1674, the work disappeared. When it was found in 1823, translated and published, it became clear that Milton was an Arian anti-trinitarian. In 1675, Herbert Croft, the Bishop of Hereford, in a work entitled THE NAKED TRUTH, argued that agreement upon forms and ceremonies is not essential, that non-Episcopal ordinations are valid, and repeated the ancient appeal for religious tolerance buttressed by a commitment to avoid disputed and uncertain doctrines.

It was inevitable that in time the Church of England would find it necessary to deal with the doctrinal issues which had been ignored for so long. The impetus for this consideration came from Thomas Firman. Firman was born in 1632, and made his fortune as a woolen dealer. He had been associated with the Puritans and then became an Independent. A supporter of John Biddle, he had once entertained Biddle as a houseguest for a period of two months. After Biddle's death, Firman focused his concerns on philanthropic interests. In 1662 he raised money to aid the Polish Socinians exiled from their homes. In 1681 he raised funds for Polish Calvinists, for French Huguenots and for Irish Protestant Refugees. He also assisted victims of the plague, of the London fire, and people imprisoned for debt. His philanthropy made him known and respected by many of the clergy of the established church. His involvement with the Independents had made him a part of the Unitarianism that was silently growing inside the Church of England and outside it.

In 1687, Firman funded the publication of A HISTORY OF THE UNITARIANS CALLED ALSO SOCINIANS, written by Stephen Nye and edited by Henry Hedworth. This was the first in a series of publications that would be called The Unitarian Tracts. Other titles included BRIEF NOTES ON THE ATHANASIAN CREED and FAITH OF ONE GOD ASSERTED AND DEFENDED. Also published in the series were letters between Nye and Firman.

The effect of the tracts was to kindle the Trinitarian Controversy within the Church of England. Beginning in 1690, there were five years of debate on the subject at Oxford. The controversy served to reveal at least two camps within the Anglican church: the "real trinitarians," those who believed that the Trinity was a literally true description of God, and the "nominal trinitarians," those who saw the Doctrine of the Trinity as a useful symbol, but not an essential understanding of the nature of God. The majority seemed to find itself in the nominalist camp. Many crypto-Unitarians felt that this interpretation provided sufficient room for their consciences and withdrew from the controversy.

In many ways, this was what Thomas Firman had intended. It had not been his hope that the entire Anglican Church would become Unitarian. Nor was he interested in splitting Unitarians off from the established church. His goal was modest—to secure sufficient latitude in interpretation to permit Unitarians to live comfortably within the Church of England. Indeed, he seems to have thought of Unitarianism as a Fraternity within the established church. When he died in 1697, he believed that he had accomplished that dream.

That the battle was not completely won, however, was signaled in the Act of Toleration of 1689. Under James II, it was decreed that dissenters could now hold public worship. However, Catholics and deniers of the Trinity were specifically excluded from the toleration that the act offered. It would not be until 1813 that toleration would be extended to these groups. What is more, in 1697, the year of Firman's death, one Thomas Aikenhead was hanged under Scottish Law for denying the trinity. This would be the last execution for heresy in Great Britain.

Nonetheless, Arian, Socinian, Unitarian thought continued to grow and develop. Isaac Newton in a work written in 1690, but not published until 1754 concluded that scripture support of the Doctrine of the Trinity is too corrupt to be relied upon. In many ways, this work reveals him to have been a Unitarian in the modern sense of the word. In 1695 John Locke published THE REASONABLENESS OF CHRISTIANITY AS DELIVERED IN SCRIPTURE. In this work, Locke argues that true revelation cannot be incompatible with reason and he advocates the broadest possible tolerance, thus demonstrating the influence of Socinianism from Holland upon his thought. Nonetheless, in 1698 Unitarians were officially barred from all public office.

The Trinitarian Controversy was ended in 1697 by order of the King. However, that did not end debate within the church. On the heels of the debate that had sought to define and explain the Trinity, came the Arian Controversy, which aimed at revising the doctrines concerning the person of Christ and the creeds of the church. At the center of this controversy were the so-called Cambridge Platonists, a group of University leaders who saw reason, morals and piety as the central concerns of religion and who insisted that minor doctrinal differences are unimportant.

Among these leaders was William Whiston, who held that primitive Christianity had been Arian in its theology and who sought to restore it in the Church of England. To this end, he revised the Book of Common Prayer to reflect primitive Christianity as he understood it, and began an effort to remove the Athanasian Creed from the worship of the church. He had few followers, but his efforts served to open the question concerning the person of Christ and the validity of the creeds. Ultimately he would be driven from the Church of England and from his chair at the University for his beliefs.

A second leader of the movement was Samuel Clarke. Clarke, who had served as Chaplain to Queen Anne, faced a moment of decision in 1709 when he was a candidate for a doctorate. The law required that in order to receive his degree or any advancement in the church, he must, on each occasion, resubscribe to the Articles of Faith of the Church of England. Clarke found himself uneasy and deeply troubled, but eventually subscribed with reservations. He came away from the experience determined to study the matter further. The study left him unable to affirm the Doctrine of the Trinity. In 1712 he published SCRIPTURE DOCTRINE OF THE TRINITY, and from that time on, he refused any new positions or preferments which would require that he resubscribe to the Articles of Faith. For his own use, he revised the Book of Common Prayer. For others, troubled as he had been, Clarke urged what came to be known as "the Arian subscription." This was a practice which argued, "in this matter (i.e. the Trinity) 'every person may agree to such forms whenever he can, in any sense at all, reconcile them with scripture.'"[21] In other words, if one's private interpretation of doctrines permitted resubscription, there was no need to be concerned that others might have a different interpretation.

Parliament examined Clarke's writings, and called their author to answer for them. Clarke offered an adroit defense and Parliament was satisfied. However, regardless of his advice to others, Clarke accepted no further preferments within the church. His Arian subscription functioned to quiet the controversy, giving many people with tender consciences the room to exist within the established church. But while the controversy faded away, its lasting effect was a growing laxity concerning creeds and liturgy.

The development of Unitarianism in England is not defined only by controversies within the established church. Rather, Unitarianism as a permanent movement, would emerge out of a dialectic between the Church of England and the nonconformist, dissenting congregations which had refused to remain within the Church of England. Central to that development among the Dissenters was Thomas Emlyn (1663-1741). Emlyn was educated for the Presbyterian ministry, and during his training was infected with Arian opinions as a result of discussions with friends and associates. In 1691 he was called to the Wood Street Church in Dublin as associate minister.

In this role, Emlyn was much loved by the congregation, especially for his preaching and for his pastoral work. For eleven years he managed to avoid controversy and to serve the congregation well. Eventually, however, a member of the congregation noted that in all that time Emlyn had never made any reference to the trinity in his sermons. Emlyn responded by acknowledging his Arianism, and offered to resign. The congregation, unwilling to lose him urged him to take a leave of absence instead.

In his absence, critics of Emlyn's theology mounted a fierce attack on him. In response, the cleric wrote AN HUMBLE INQUIRY INTO THE SCRIPTURE ACCOUNT OF JESUS CHRIST. Published in 1702, the book resulted in its author being arrested for blasphemy. Tried and found guilty, Emlyn was fined one thousand pounds and jailed for a year. Unable to pay his fine, he remained in jail for two years until at last his fine was reduced and paid. (Emlyn was the last person jailed for denial of the Trinity in Great Britain). His case aroused much sympathy in London, where it was seen as a clear instance of injustice. Nonetheless, Emlyn, despite his obvious gifts, could find no congregation, the Westminster Confession having been made mandatory for dissenting clergy in 1705. He moved to London where he gathered a small congregation. He was the first minister in Britain to assume the Unitarian name despite the fact that he remained Arian in his theology. His book would continue to have significant influence on the development of Unitarianism on both sides of the Atlantic.

Emlyn had been Presbyterian, but the Dissenting or Nonconforming Protestants included other groups as well. Over time, their relative liberal or conservative positions tended to shift as they interacted with each other in complex ways. Thus, after the Act of Toleration of 1689, the Presbyterians tended to be the largest, wealthiest of the Dissenting sects and were moving from Calvinism toward freedom of belief. Because of their class, they tended to be most influenced by debates within the Church of England, and they were not eager to submit to creeds. The Independents, who had once been most eager to support tolerance had become the most conservative, were strict Calvinists, but most democratic in their practice. The Baptists were drawn from the humbler social classes but were the most tolerant in doctrinal matters.

Because their children were excluded from schools and universities unless they were prepared to subscribe to the Articles of Faith, Dissenters had established their own Academies in England. The Dissenting Academies, taught by clergymen, offered a better education than Oxford or Cambridge at the time. They tended to be creedless, encouraging open and free discussion. It was here that ministers for Nonconforming congregations were prepared—ministers who would lead many of the Dissenters in the direction of liberal religion.

It was in Exeter that the debate over the Doctrine of the Trinity emerged again. James Peirce had been called to the dissenters Chapel at Exeter in 1713. Peirce was a Presbyterian who had been influenced by Whiston and Clarke and the Arian controversy. Several years after his arrival, discussion concerning the trinity began in the congregation, with some members whispering that even the minister questioned the doctrine. In 1718 members requested sermons concerning the deity of Christ. Peirce agreed reluctantly, and as a result of his sermons, the issue became public. The Exeter assembly of ministers met to consider the matter, and eventually declared for the Doctrine of the Trinity. Nonetheless, Arianism continued to grow.[22] Peirce was ejected from his pulpit by the proprietors of the chapel, but rather than retiring quietly, he established a new church—the first congregation devoted to anti-trinitarian worship to survive to the present.

Conservatives in Exeter wrote to dissenting ministers in London, seeking advice on how to respond to the growing Arianism. In response, twenty-five ministers met to discuss the matter. The group was most reluctant to intervene. However, they were equally concerned to avoid a schism among the Dissenters given the fact that Parliament was considering legislation concerning religious dissidents. Therefore, the group concluded that, while there may be differences serious enough to justify a rift between the clergy and the people, congregations themselves should determine what these differences are. Finally, the meeting urged a conciliatory spirit. In effect, the advice was that the local congregation should solve its own problems as quietly as possible.

Conservative ministers, however, were uncomfortable with this political response to what they saw as a theological question. They urged another meeting to determine what doctrinal advice might be added to the procedural advice. Meeting at Salters' Hall, the group, consisting of eighty Presbyterians, forty Independents and thirty Baptists, was presented with a conservative proposal that the Doctrine of the Trinity is the center of Christian faith. The debate was long and heated, but eventually the motion was defeated by a vote of 57-53.

The meeting was adjourned and scheduled to reconvene on March 3, 1719. Both sides used the time to rally forces, and when the meeting resumed, another attempt to add a statement of faith was ruled out of order. Eventually a paper was submitted containing an article on the Trinity from the Church of England and the Westminster Confession. Sixty of the delegates signed the statement and then withdrew to organize their own meeting. Seventy-three refused to subscribe, but agreed to send the recommendations concerning procedure to Exeter, along with a letter affirming the Doctrine of the Trinity and justifying their refusal to sign or require any creed. The result of the Salters' Hall controversy was that the Dissenting Protestants split into two groups, the Subscribing and the Nonsubscribing churches. It should be understood that the issue between them, while it began with debate over the Trinity, soon became a difference over freedom of conscience. The Salters' Hall meeting was the first gathering of ministers in England to call for freedom of conscience.

It is difficult to trace the history of the Nonsubscribing churches, given the fact that they were not really a denomination, but rather a scattering of independent congregations. They drew their members from the wealthy and educated classes, their ministers were able, dedicated, and well-educated. While they had no unified program and no central leadership, they seemed to follow a common path of development. Beginning with a commitment to freedom, they regarded the Doctrine of the Trinity at first as not essential, then unimportant, and then ignored it. In many cases, Arianism gradually evolved into Unitarianism.

While these developments were occurring among the Dissidents, Dr. Clarke's compromise, the Arian Subscription, had quieted debate within the Church of England. A few, like Dr. Clarke simply declined any elevation to higher office and thus avoided the need to resubscribe the Articles of Faith. Others affirmed the articles with whatever personal reservations or interpretations made it possible for them to do so. However, there was growing discontent beneath the surface at a process that seemed less than honest and candid.

In 1749, an anonymous work entitled A FREE AND CANDID DISQUISITION RELATING TO THE CHURCH OF ENGLAND appeared. The author proposed a new translation of the Bible, major changes to the liturgy of the church and abolition of the practice of resubscription. This proposal inaugurated a twenty-year discussion of the creeds and practices of the English church. Central to the debate that followed was the Doctrine of the Trinity and the creed attributed to its greatest protagonist, St. Athanasius. Church law required that the Athanasian Creed be used in all services of the church. It did not, however, prescribe how it was to be used. In one parish, the minister had it sung to a popular hunting tune. In another, it was introduced with this preface: "Brethren, this is the creed of St. Athanasius; but God forbid it should be the creed of any other man."[23] By and large, the bishops chose to ignore these modest protests.

No one took the FREE AND CANDID DISQUISITION more seriously than the Rev. William Robertson. After reading the proposals for change in the church, Robertson realized that he could not continue his ministry. He laid his scruples before his bishop, who simply did not respond to his concerns. In 1764, at the age of 60, Robertson resigned his post and became a teacher in a grammar school. Two years later, he published a work in which he explained why one should hesitate to subscribe to the vaguely worded and unclear terms of creeds and statements of faith.

Jarred into action, by the controversy surrounding the issue of subscription, and by the insistence of the church hierarchy that the resolution of the crisis would require action by the civil authorities, Rev. Francis Stone proposed that Parliament be petitioned to repeal the practice of subscription. In 1771, the Feathers Tavern Association was formed to push the petition. After months of effort, the

Association was able to obtain only 250 signatures on the petition. Predictably, when the petition was presented in 1772, Parliament rejected it by vote of 217-71.

The failure of the Feathers Tavern Petition seemed to leave things largely unchanged. However, it was a momentous event for Theophilus Lindsey. Early in his ministry Lindsey had had doubts about the Doctrine of the Trinity and had soon moved past Arianism to Unitarianism. After 1763 he had decided he could not resubscribe the Articles of Faith, so he would accept no new post or honors. He continued to minister to a his small congregation, preaching twice each Sunday, and organizing a Sunday evening school for one hundred boys, focused on a curriculum of Bible study.

As the years passed, he found himself less and less comfortable with his relation to the creeds of the church. When he became aware of Robertson's resignation, his conscience troubled him even more. In this state of mind, he met Joseph Priestley and William Turner, both dissenting ministers. When he discussed his situation with them, both advised him to stay where he was and to revise the liturgy as he saw fit.

It was good advice, but Lindsey was not comfortable with it. He looked to the Feathers Tavern Petition as a way to avoid having to make a difficult choice. When the petition failed, Lindsey determined that he must resign his post at the end of the year. His friends tried to dissuade him, but he would not be deterred. In November of 1773, at fifty years of age, he sent his resignation to the Bishop.

Lindsey received offers of positions with various Dissenting congregations, but he had another goal in mind. With the support of his wife, he sold his property and set out for London, determined to establish a Unitarian Congregation in that city, hoping that by his action he could entice other like-minded clergy to withdraw from the Church of England. En route to London, he discovered Clarke's revised prayer book which he copied for later use. In 1774, using funds gathered from friends and Dissenters, Lindsey rented an auction room on Essex Street and turned it into a chapel. He created a liturgy based on Clarke's work, and held his first service on April 17, 1774. Among those attending that first service was Benjamin Franklin, who was frequently in Lindsay's congregation when he was in London.

Three years later, the permanence of Linsdey's chapel seemed assured. The Essex Street property was purchased and remodeled into a large chapel with the minister's residence on the ground floor. Five years after that, Lindsey published AN HISTORICAL VIEW OF UNITARIAN DOCTRINE, a work that traced Unitarian history from Poland and Transylvania to England. That same year Rev. John Disney, an Anglican Clergyman, became Lindsey's colleague at Essex Street.

Lindsey had hoped that his example would induce other Unitarians to withdraw from the Church of England. When Disney resigned his position at the Essex Street Chapel in 1805, he was followed by Thomas Belsham, a Dissenter. In many ways, that was the end of Lindsey's dream of a Unitarian secession from the Anglican Church. From that point on, the Unitarians would be firmly in the ranks of the Dissenting churches. Lindsey died in 1808; by 1810 there were twenty congregations bearing the Unitarian name; and by 1813 the Trinity Act finally freed Unitarians of civil disabilities.

This development of Unitarianism as a separate movement was supplemented by developments among the Dissenters, especially the non-subscribing Presbyterians. After the passage of the Act of Toleration there had been a marked decline in the vigor and the vitality of the Dissenting groups, almost as if lack of oppression resulted in a lost sense of mission. This decline was particularly true of the more liberal Presbyterians, who were seen as coldly intellectual and appeared on the very verge of extinction. The man who would reverse this drift and give the movement a new sense of mission and promise was Joseph Priestley.

Priestley was born in 1733, and reared in a Calvinist home. Like many young people of the time, he was educated by Dissenting ministers—at Daventry Academy, where he betrayed an early interest in religion. At the Academy he came under the influence of two tutors, one an orthodox Calvinist, the other inclined to heresy. The student body was about evenly divided between orthodoxy and heresy. Already unorthodox as a child, indeed so unorthodox that he was refused admission to the Calvinist church because of his rejection of the church's teachings on predestination and original sin, Priestley entered the Academy as a moderate Calvinist, and left it an Arian.

Despite a pronounced stammer, young Priestley entered the ministry as an assistant minister in Suffolk. Along with his regular duties he continued his study of the Bible, and grew steadily more radical in his views. During this time he abandoned all belief in the doctrine of the atonement, and surrendered his faith in the divine inspiration of the scriptures. He left the ministry for a while to teach languages and literature at Warrington Academy. During his years at the academy he expanded the scope of his teaching to include history, government, logic and economics. It was also during these years that he formed a friendship with Benjamin Franklin.

Priestley returned to the ministry in 1767, when he accepted a call to serve the congregation at Leeds. At this point in his life, he moved from his early Arian views and embraced Socinianism. He founded the THEOLOGICAL REPOSITORY, an occasional publication for the discussion of important issues. He also published a text for the instruction of the young and various pamphlets for his congregation, urging daily family worship and the education of children in their faith, and defining church discipline. He wrote a number of tracts defending and explaining to the public at large the message of liberal religion. As if he had not enough to do, it was in this period that he began his study of chemistry and in 1774 discovered oxygen. The world best remembers Priestley as a scientist. Priestley thought of his science as "a theologian's pastime."

In 1773 Priestley accepted the position of librarian to the Earl of Shelburne, a post which allowed him freedom to meet with leading dissenters and to follow his many interests. Seven years later, he was called as minister to Birmingham's New Meeting. While in Birmingham, Priestley completed CORRUPTIONS OF CHRISTIANITY, a work in which he used his vast scholarship to demonstrate that primitive Christianity had been Unitarian and that all deviations from that standard must be seen as corruptions. The book provoked a strong response and eight years of debate, one contribution to which was a four-volume work by Priestley entitled HISTORY OF EARLY OPINIONS CONCERNING JESUS CHRIST.

By this time, Priestley was the acknowledged leader of the Unitarian dissenters, and Nonsubscribing Unitarianism was a revitalized movement. Nonsubscribing congregations increased in number and exhibited renewed zeal and devotion to their cause. The progress of Unitarianism in England was interrupted, however, by the emergence of the French Revolution as a political issue. Priestley and the Unitarians, along with other liberals, who had been supporters of the American Revolution, were early supporters of the political upheaval across the channel, seeing in it the promise of a humanity freed from the shackles of despotism and superstition. Conservatives and orthodox leaders saw only irreligious madness and murder as peasants rose up against their betters and sought to overthrow the social order. In the end, as England became more and more frightened by the turmoil across the channel, Priestley and the Unitarians would be denounced as enemies of church and state.

In 1791 a mob attacked and burned Priestley's church, library, and laboratory. Fearing for his own safety, Priestley fled to London. Three years later, he sailed to America, where he established a Unitarian Church in Philadelphia before making his permanent home in Northumberland. Priestley continued his radical progress throughout his life, coming to believe that worship of Christ is nothing more than idolatry, that the soul is not immortal but is simply a function of the body, and that the church is little more than "an overgrown fungus on the body of true Christianity.[24] His legacy to English Unitarianism is to be found in the fact that he was instrumental in defining the Unitarian witness as distinct from that of other dissenters. His radical views created an unbridgeable schism between the Unitarians and other forms of dissent. More than this, he bequeathed to them a conviction that Christian doctrine is not fixed, but must continue to develop, requiring a strong commitment to the intellectual process and a reliance on reason.

After Priestley's departure for America, the liberal dissenters were in disarray. Many of the Academies were closed. Lindsey, the great old man of the movement was aged, the conservative tide in the country was running strong and there was no clear successor to Priestley. Into this leadership vacuum stepped Thomas Belsham.

Belsham had been born in 1750. He began his career as an orthodox Calvinist teacher. In teaching Christian doctrine to his students, he gradually convinced himself to embrace Unitarianism. In 1779 he attended a service at the Essex Street Chapel and discovered "it was possible for a Socinian to be a good man."[25] In 1791 he was instrumental in organizing the Unitarian Society for Promoting Christian Knowledge and Practice by Virtue of the Distribution of Books—better known as the Unitarian Book Society. The ground rules of the society were drawn to unite those who were strict believers in the unity of God and the simple humanity of Jesus. The practical effect was to exclude Arians and thus begin the separation of Unitarianism from Arianism.

In 1794 Belsham was called to the Unitarian church at Hackney, and then in 1805 was called to succeed Lindsey at the Essex Street church. By this time he had become the acknowledge leader of the Unitarian movement in a time of new and important undertakings. The first Unitarian periodical, THE MONTHLY REPOSITORY, was established; for two decades it was successful in knitting together the Unitarian movement throughout the country. The same period saw the establishment of The Unitarian Fund for Promoting Unitarianism by Means of Popular Preaching. Among those supported by the fund was Rev. Richard Wright, who gathered churches among the laboring classes.

In 1808, Belsham released an improved version of the New Testament, which was promptly dubbed the Unitarian New Testament. The following year saw establishment of the Unitarian Tract Society that published materials promoting and supporting Unitarian views.

In 1816 the tranquility of the Unitarian movement was shattered by the Wolverhampton case—a legal challenge to the rights of a number of Unitarian Congregations to the property they had been using. St. John's Chapel, Wolverhampton, had been established in 1701 for use by Protestant Dissenters. The congregation, undoubtedly orthodox at the time of the founding of the chapel had, over time, become Unitarian. Conservatives insisted that donation of the chapel had been for Christian worship, that the founders had not been Unitarian, and therefore, the chapel did not belong to the Unitarian congregation now using it. To the dismay of the Unitarians, after years of litigation, the courts held for the conservatives.

In response to the threat this legal decision represented, Belsham organized the Unitarian Association for Protecting the Civil Rights of Unitarians. The focus of this organization, founded in 1819, was to work to protect the rights of Unitarians to the property they had been accustomed to use, and to establish the right of Unitarian clergy to perform weddings, a rite exclusively within the domain of the Anglican clergy. The Association would succeed in winning the rights of Unitarians to marriages by their own clergy in 1836, but the right to property would not be secured until the Unitarians had suffered another profound shock.

The decision in the Wolverhampton case was echoed in a similar suit known as the Lady Hewley Case. In 1842, conservatives sought to gain legal control of a fund Unitarians had been administering that was the bequest of one Lady Hewley. The fund had been established in 1704 to aid ministers. Lady Hewley had not prescribed any doctrinal conditions for the use of the fund. However, conservatives successfully argued that since Lady Hewley was not a Unitarian, Unitarians had no right to the fund they had been administering. The conservatives won the case, but lost the issue, when Parliament responded by passing the Dissenters Chapel Bill in 1844. This bill established that any demonstration of undisputed use of property for twenty-five years by a congregation would constitute a valid claim to that property, thus protecting many congregations from claims that would dispossess them.

Near the end of Belsham's life the need for a body to co-ordinate all the activities of the denomination was so clear that the Unitarian Fund and the Civil Rights Association were merged to create the British and Foreign Unitarian Association in May of 1825. The next year, the Unitarian Book Society also merged into the new structure. When he died four years later, Belsham left behind a well-established religious moment. Over his years of leadership, he had created and provided the means by which scattered liberal dissenters could be forged into an on-going denomination. When the Unitarians withdrew from the London Dissenting Ministers Association in 1844, they severed their last link with Orthodoxy. Under the influence of James Martineau, they continued their journey, abandoning scripture as the only basis of faith, discarding belief in miracles, insisting that Jesus was fully human with no special messianic role, and that reason is the supreme authority in religion.

English Unitarianism exhibited an ability to attract people from a wide variety of backgrounds. In Lancashire in 1806 one Joseph Cooke was expelled from the Methodists. The congregations he had served withdrew in support of him. Cooke, though he never himself became an Arian or a Unitarian, led them in a program of Bible study that resulted in their coming to Unitarian convictions on their own. A Methodist Unitarian Association made up of lay preachers and congregations composed of poverty-stricken working people was formed and maintained an existence until 1844, when it merged with the Unitarian Association. In 1822 Rammohun Roy created a Unitarian related movement that evolved into the Brahmo Samaj in India. In 1826 fifty congregations of General Baptists joined the Unitarian Association.

By 1900 there were three hundred and sixty Unitarian Churches in England, and a movement of Nonsubscribing Presbyterians in Ireland. In more recent years Unitarianism has experienced the same decline in vitality which has afflicted much of organized religion in England. Toward the end of the century, Unitarianism in England is seeking renewal and revitalization that will carry it into the new millennium.

UNITARIANISM IN THE UNITED STATES

As was the case with Polish Socinianism, and Transylvanian and English Unitarianism, the development on the North American continent was highly shaped and influenced by the political and religious context in which it evolved. Direct influences from European anti-trinitarian movements were few, and difficult to trace. Before 1800, there were no Socinian books, and few, if any, Unitarian works in the library at Harvard College.[26] There is a record that two Polish Socinians settled in Georgia in 1738, but they disappeared from history without leaving a trace. In 1803, a preacher from Holland, who may have been Socinian, founded a church in Barneveld, NY, a church which is still in existence, and is currently a member of the Unitarian Universalist Association. In 1785 Theophilus Lindsey's Revised Prayer Book influenced King's Chapel, when it embraced Unitarianism. And, as we have already indicated, Joseph Priestley, upon his arrival on this continent in 1794, founded two Unitarian Churches in Pennsylvania, one of which is still in existence. Occasional Unitarians were among the immigrants to Canada in the first quarter of the nineteenth century, but the first permanent congregation was not established in that country until 1842.[27] None of these influences represented a major force in the development of Unitarianism in America.

American Unitarianism was rooted in New England, and was a consequence of the same religious conflicts that shaped the Protestant Reformation in England and gave rise to Unitarianism there. Indeed, American Unitarianism and English Unitarianism developed simultaneously but were largely independent of each other. The seeds of that development were present in the first impulses that planted English colonies in Massachusetts.

The colonists who founded Plymouth were composed of separatists—radical Protestants who refused the Elizabethan compromise of the Church of England, and were determined to worship apart from the established church. In order to pursue their religious vision, the community had emigrated to Holland. Fearful that their children would fall under the influence of their Dutch neighbors and forget their English heritage, the Pilgrims, as they have come to be known, came to North America, seeking to build a Zion in the wilderness, a place where true Christianity might flourish unimpeded by worldly neighbors or oppressive government restrictions. By the nature of their experience, they tended to be a community bounded by covenant with each other and with God, but without a strong political tradition by which they were to be governed. And, reflecting their sojourn in Holland, they also tended to be more tolerant than their neighbors in Massachusetts Bay.

Puritans out of the Anglican Church created the Massachusetts Bay Colony. They were possessed of a dream that one day, the Anglican Church would come to its senses, do away with its Episcopal hierarchy, purge its liturgy and practices of all vestiges of Catholic influence, and become pure and wholesome. Some of the Puritans saw themselves as exiles who had come to Massachusetts temporarily to keep the vision alive in the wilderness until the time came when the political climate would permit them to return home and participate in the purification of the English Church. They never pretended to be tolerant of error in the church; indeed, the strict Calvinism of church members was assumed and only members of the church were granted political rights. Nor did these colonists hesitate to institute laws against heresy, aimed at Baptists, Quakers, Catholics, Episcopalians, et al. But because they saw their situation as temporary, they felt little need to hedge their religious community about with creedal restrictions. Nor did they feel the need for an elaborate structure of church governance. They, after all, were the saints of God, awaiting the call to come home and reform the Church in England.

The unintended consequence of this mind-set was to leave open the door for gradual and subtle changes in faith as the years dragged on, and the dream of return receded, and new generations, no longer fired by the same enthusiasm for purity of doctrine, arrived on the scene. In the early period, as congregations were gathered among the settlers, there was no creed required of church members. Rather there were covenants in which people pledged, with God's help, to live a Christian life in accordance with the teaching of the scriptures. It was assumed that a church member would have had some personal religious experience, some sense of election in which his spiritual life and participation in the church was grounded, but there was no standard for assuring the validity of that experience. What creeds there were functioned as standards of belief, but were not understood as binding on the various churches.

In very short order, as the first generation of settlers gave way to succeeding generations that were born in exile, the faith which had brought this people to a new land began to change in subtle ways. As the fervor of the first generation failed to be communicated to the children, the sense of being exiles longing to go home was replaced by a sense of being at home in the only world they had ever known, and temporary expedience became cherished custom. The scope of those changes can be seen in a variety of ways. In 1648, representatives of the churches in Massachusetts met to settle the form of government under which their congregations would operate. The motive for this meeting was a fear that the growing Puritan power in England would impose a presbyterian polity upon the New England congregations. The result of the meeting was the Cambridge Platform, which established what had been a temporary expedient, congregational polity, as the permanent structure under which the churches would be governed. The dream that motivated Puritanism in England was quickly supplanted by a desire to retain the freedom and the independence that the exigencies of life in the wilderness had made familiar and comfortable and right.

Nor was the change within the New England churches confined to matters of polity. Within one generation, preachers and writers began to complain about a growing laxity of doctrine within the colony. By 1654, that complaint had become more specific as Edward Johnson, in WONDER WORKING PROVIDENCE complained of growing Arianism and Arminianism.[28] What is more, as the first generation was replaced by the second and third generations, fewer and fewer people were able to witness to a personal experience of grace, and thus fewer and fewer people were willing to assert the claim that would permit them to qualify as members of the community of saints who comprised the church. The response of the churches to this situation was to institute the "Half-way Covenant," which permitted the children of church members, who lived moral and upright lives to participate in the life of the church, excepting participation in the Lord's Supper. In this way, the church itself acknowledged that the Puritan ideal that had brought their forebears to New England was eroding.

Nonetheless, by a variety of means, the leaders of the colony were able to slow the process and to control, in large measure the degree of outside influence until 1691. At that point Parliament voided the Colony's Charter and Massachusetts became a crown colony answerable to the government in London. With this change, Puritans lost control of the colony, and the ideas of liberal writers popular in England, began to flow into New England. Locke and Milton, Whiston and Clarke began to be read in the New World, and with their books came echoes of the debates and controversies which were troubling the English church. Whiston and Clarke brought the trinitarian controversy to the attention of Massachusetts churchmen. The news of Emlyn's troubles in Dublin crossed the Atlantic, as did reports of the conflict at Exeter and the Salters' Hall controversy. Arians on both sides of the Atlantic became aware of each other's existence, and correspondence sprang up between them. The effect of all this was to speed the process by which the Calvinist constitution of the colony was undermined.

Watching these developments, more conservative clergymen become increasingly concerned that they were witnessing a disastrous decline in the intensity of religious faith. However there seemed to be little they could do but view with alarm and lament at how the mighty had fallen. In 1722, Cotton Mather echoed many of his colleagues in lamenting that the preachers in the colony were neglecting to "preach Christ." The sense of a falling away from the true faith, grew and troubled many clergy and lay people as well.

At the moment when it seemed that there was no hope of stopping the slide into religious laxity and indifference, the churches of Massachusetts were gripped by a revival known as The Great Awakening. It began in 1734, when the Reverend Jonathan Edwards began preaching powerfully passionate sermons to his congregation in Northampton, stirring his listeners to an emotional and deeply felt repentance. From that point, the revival spread throughout the colony and up and down the Atlantic coast. Indeed, some historians have suggested that in many ways the Great Awakening was the first truly national experience for Americans. The fervor touched off in New England, spread through the middle Atlantic region, and into the South.[29]

The immediate effect of the Great Awakening was to arouse a renewed interest in religion, and a deepened commitment to old values. So great were the opportunities it represented that a variety of preachers were caught up in the enterprise. Some of them, like Edwards, were settled in parishes, but many others were itinerants, moving from place to place, stirring up religious enthusiasm, encouraging emotional excesses, nurturing a fanatical spirit in those touched by the revivalist fervor, and everywhere encouraging a reactionary dogmatism as the standard of religious truth.

The long term effect of this effort to revive and reinvigorate the old Calvinist consensus would be a permanent division between those who saw in the revival the hand of God, and those who, shaped by the growing liberalism of recent decades, saw only madness and raw emotion and who preferred a religion of reason and sobriety. In many places the lines of conflict were drawn between the settled ministers and the itinerants. Among the most famous of the itinerant ministers who enlisted in the cause of the Awakening was George Whitefield, who came from England to exploit the opportunities of the revival. Whitefield, a dynamic preacher, was undiplomatic enough to refer to the New England clergy as "dumb dogs, half devils and half beasts, spiritually blind and leading people to hell."[30]

While many of the liberal clergy spoke out against the excesses of the revival, by and large they refused to enter into controversy with Whitefield. Rather, they simply closed their pulpits to him, refusing to offer him a platform in their communities. Increasingly, they united in defining reason and tolerance as the basis of religion. To bolster themselves and to find sources of support, many of them turned to liberal books and colleagues for intellectual sustenance. The inevitable result of the process was a deepening division between those who were caught up in the revival and those who resisted and opposed it. By 1750, some thirty ministers were said to be unsound in doctrine—Arians, Socinians, Arminians or some combination. For the most part, these ministers were accused of neglecting the Doctrine of the Deity of Christ. And over time, those accusations would prove to be accurate.

The process of liberalization in the New England Churches was gradual, almost insensible. Preachers did not challenge doctrines with which they had difficulty. Rather, they simply ceased to emphasize those doctrines; then they left them out of sermons and services, and only after a period of time did they consciously abandon them. A number of factors eased this process. First of all, congregational polity, which left control of the church in the hands of the local congregation, provided no mechanism for effective oversight or discipline. What is more, the prevailing custom among the New England congregations was that ministers were settled for life. Thus, many ministers had the opportunity to shape a congregation's expectations, customs and beliefs over several generations.

Ebenezer Gay (1696-1787) served the church at Hingham for sixty-nine years. His habit was to abstain from controversy in preaching. However, he intensely disliked the emotionalism of the Great Awakening. He sought a religion rooted in reason and judgement. The last two generations that experienced his ministry heard nothing of the old Calvinist doctrines from his pulpit. Under his quiet, effective leadership, the congregation at Hingham became liberal, quietly and without fully recognizing what had happened.

Similarly, Charles Chauncey (1705-1787) served First Church in Boston for sixty years. He, too, opposed the Great Awakening, and under his leadership, First Church became a liberal church. Indeed, not only did Chauncy abandon much of Calvinism, he ably defended universal salvation.

Jonathan Mayhew (1720-1766), minister of the West Church in Boston, went a step further. He was clear and outspoken in his rejection of the Doctrine of the Trinity. As early as 1753, Mayhew preached the strict unity of God. He argued that it was the duty of all to approach religion in the spirit of free inquiry, and that there can be no greater authority than private judgment in religion. Therefore he opposed all creeds. His preaching often focused on political questions, resulting in his being described as the father of civil and religious liberty in Massachusetts. The church he served supported their minister fully, and, while it never took the Unitarian name, The West Church in Boston may well be called the first Unitarian church in America.

This growing liberalism was aided and abetted by the reprinting of Emlyn's "HUMBLE INQUIRY" in America in 1756. A year later a group of New Hampshire churches revised their catechism to delete all references to the trinity. While other ministers and congregations were not willing to go as far as Mayhew or the New Hampshire churches, nonetheless Arianism was growing quietly among the New England clergy and in the Congregational Churches.

At this point, the focus of the story shifts from the Congregational Churches to the oldest Episcopal Congregation in New England. King's Chapel had been established in 1686, and functioned as an Anglican Church until it was closed in 1776, a casualty of the American Revolution. From 1777 to 1783, the building was used by the congregation of Old South Church, whose own building had been appropriated by the British Army to stable horses. In 1782-83, the remaining congregation of King's Chapel resolved to recover its property and resume services.

The immediate problem facing them was a shortage of Anglican clergy in the wake of the defeat of the British and the establishment of American independence. In 1782, the congregation asked James Freeman, a recent Harvard graduate who was Congregationalist in background, to serve as reader. He was granted permission to use his own sermons or to read sermons by others. Significantly, he was also granted permission to omit the Athanasian Creed and to make such other changes in the services, as he thought best.

On this basis, services resumed under Freeman's leadership in 1783. After a time, Freeman grew increasingly uneasy about the Doctrine of the Trinity, and eventually announced that he could no longer use the Book of Common Prayer because of that doctrine. Rather than give offense to the congregation or create a division, he offered to resign. Instead, the congregation requested that he preach a series of sermons on the matter. The sermons must have been effective, for in the end the congregation endorsed Freeman's views on the subject.

In 1785, Freeman and the King's Chapel Congregation revised the Book of Common Prayer, following the liturgy used by Theophilus Lindsey at the Essex Street Chapel in London. At the same time, the congregation sought to have Freeman ordained. The Anglican bishops refused permission for the ordination. Faced with an impasse, and aware of the polity of neighboring congregational churches, which recognized the authority of the local congregation to ordain ministers of its own choosing, King's Chapel chose to ordain James Freeman in 1787.

The response was predictable. King's Chapel was expelled from fellowship with the Anglican Church, and was welcomed into fellowship by the Congregational ministers of Boston. Freeman, accepted and honored by the Boston Clergy, began a correspondence with Priestley, Lindsey and Belsham, leaders of Unitarianism in England. In this way, the first Episcopal Church in New England became Unitarian.

Freeman's example and influence was felt beyond his own church. His correspondence with English Unitarians resulted in Lindsey sending books on Unitarianism to Harvard College. Three old, prosperous congregations in Salem, a community made up of people engaged in foreign commerce and therefore accustomed to contacts with non-Christians, had developed a spirit of broad and liberal tolerance and thus were well prepared for the move into Unitarianism. John Prince, minister of First Church had amassed a library of English Unitarian Books. William Bentley, Minister of East Church had been a classmate of James Freeman at Harvard, and an early follower of Priestley. Not surprisingly, he was a pronounced

Unitarian. So was Dr. Thomas Barnard, minister of North Church, who was once accosted by a parishioner who commented, "I never heard you preach a sermon on the Trinity," to which Dr. Barnard replied, "And you never will."[31] It is not surprising that these congregations watched events at King's Chapel with interest and approval. Nor is it surprising that all three, quietly, without controversy, almost insensibly became Unitarian.

In 1792, influenced by the teachings of Joseph Priestley, as mediated by James Freeman, a majority of the members of the Episcopal Church of Portland withdrew from that congregation and established a Unitarian Society. This church died with its minister in 1799. It has, however, the honor of being the first congregation in America to adopt the Unitarian name.

While these events were developing in New England, there were a few stirrings in the Mid-Atlantic region. As early as 1783, William Hazlitt of England was preaching Unitarianism from Maryland to Maine, with special attention to Philadelphia. A year later, Priestley's works were published in Pennsylvania. In 1794 the First Unitarian Society of New York, heavily influenced from England, was established, but it lasted only a few months.

It was not until Joseph Priestley arrived that same year that Unitarianism took any kind of permanent root in this region. Priestley spent two weeks in New York and then moved on to Philadelphia. After a brief stay he moved to Northumberland, where he held services in his home. In 1796, Priestley used the Universalist Church in Philadelphia, delivering twelve lectures on Christianity, and one sermon on Unitarianism from its pulpit. A year later the First Society of Unitarian Christians was established in Philadelphia, a church which called its first minister in 1807, and which exists to this day, claiming to be the first permanent Unitarian Church in the United States.

Important as these scattered efforts may have been, the Unitarian movement in the United States would be shaped by events in

New England, and especially in Massachusetts, where the Unitarian Controversy was about to erupt within the churches of the Standing Order. During the American Revolution, there had been little doctrinal debate within the churches. The chasm that had opened between liberals and conservatives as a result of the Great Awakening had been bridged by a common concern over the struggle for independence. When the war ended, however, there was no way to return to the status quo ante-bellum. The Revolution not only realigned political realities, it had also initiated a religious realignment. The Universalists, the Hicksite Quakers and the churches of the Christian Connection all emerged in this period. And part of this religious realignment was an ever-widening gulf between liberals and conservatives within the Congregation Churches of Massachusetts.

Alarmed by the growth of liberalism, conservatives within the churches began to demand that church members be required to subscribe to creeds and that candidates for the ministry be examined to determine if their theology be sound—proposals which were unacceptable to many liberals, and which were seen to be divisive and contrary to the freedom which was a cherished part of the heritage of the New England churches.

The liberals, on their part, looked to England and to each other for support. The Unitarians in England had supported the Americans in their struggle for independence, and they offered strong arguments in support of tolerance and in opposition to creeds. In 1790, Emlyn's HUMBLE INQUIRY was once again reprinted in America.

In 1795, Jeremy Belknap of Federal Street Church in Boston published A COLLECTION OF PSALMS AND HYMNS, a work which omitted all references to the Trinity, and the Boston churches abandoned Trinitarian doxologies in their services. Indeed, despite the conservative's attempt to erect a creedal wall in defense of orthodoxy, liberal views continue to grow and develop. By 1800, of the 200 churches east of Worcester County, 125 were liberal in their theology. Of 20 churches in Plymouth County, 18 were infected with liberalism. And 8 of the 9 churches in Boston were considered unsound on the Trinity. Harvard College, which trained the ministers for the Massachusetts churches, was considered a hot bed of heresy.

There were few disciplinary structures the conservatives could employ to combat the growing heresy. The congregational polity of the churches offered no overarching authority by which a standard could be established or deviation could be discovered and disciplined. Only the local church could act and the issue presented itself to the local congregation usually at times of crisis, when a ministerial vacancy forced it to seek a new minister. Then it was that churches would sometimes divide into evangelical and liberal camps. In the last decade of the eighteenth century several churches split over the selection of a new minister—a harbinger of coming events. Indeed, in Worcester, as early as 1784, the liberals organized a Second Parish, the first church in New England organized on the basis of complete religious liberty.

These New England liberals were not Unitarians in the English sense of the word. For many of them, Priestley's thought was far too radical. Some were still largely Arian in their thinking, while others had progressed to Unitarianism of a more conservative sort. They were distinguished by a strong dislike of controversy. They refused to be drawn into doctrinal debate, and quietly chose to ignore doctrines they found troublesome or unacceptable. In this way they presided over a slowly emerging liberalism which remained difficult to pin down and challenge—a fact which enraged conservatives who came to believe that the liberals were guilty of a deliberate conspiracy aimed at seducing the church into heresy.

The one place where doctrinal differences could be seen clearly was at the annual gathering of the Massachusetts Clergy, the Ministerial Convention, which met at the time of the May General Court. The purpose of the meeting was to discuss the state of religion in the Commonwealth and a highlight of the meeting was the annual occasional sermon. As early as 1768 these sermons had begun to give voice to the different visions of religion within Massachusetts. Much of the issue seemed to be focused around whether the Convention should be tolerant of differences, or whether it should seek a standard of orthodoxy.

After 1800, the evangelicals, under the leadership of the Rev. Jedediah Morse of Cambridge sought to force the liberal ministers from the Convention. The attempt failed, and an implicit agreement developed in which the evangelical and the liberal parties would alternate in delivering the annual Convention sermon. The effect of this effort was not to appease the two sides to the dispute, or to bring them closer together, but rather to emphasize and heighten the differences between them. Morse, the champion of orthodoxy, bided his time and waited for an opportunity to force the liberal party to declare itself.

His first opportunity came in 1803 when Dr. David Tappan, Hollis Professor of Divinity at Harvard College, died. The choice of Tappen's successor occasioned a fierce struggle between the two wings of the Congregational Church. The liberal candidate, Henry Ware, was minister at Hingham, the successor of Ebenezer Gay. Ware was known to be an Arian, but stoutly denied the evangelical charge that he was a Unitarian. The orthodox candidate was Jesse Appleton. The Corporation, a board of six charged with making the choice, was evenly divided. For more than a year the decision was debated and delayed. Eventually, in February of 1805 the Corporation, after six meetings, selected Henry Ware for the vacant post, and sent its recommendation to the Board of Overseers for confirmation. The Overseers, after a heated debate, in which Morse led the opposition, ratified the choice and Henry Ware became Hollis Professor of Divinity, largely responsible for the education of future ministers for the Massachusetts Congregational Churches.

Morse and other conservatives were so angered by this choice that they resigned from the Board of Overseers. Liberals were immediately elected to replace them. It was now clear that the liberal party had gained effective control of Harvard, and the process by which leadership of the church would be educated. Morse and the orthodox party began to cast about for a means to train orthodox clergy for evangelical pulpits. In 1808, their efforts would result in the opening of Andover Theological Seminary, overtly Calvinist, committed to a creed which professors would be required to resubscribe every five years as a guard against creeping liberalism in this bastion of orthodox thought. In many ways, this marked the final and definitive moment in the schism that had split the churches of the Standing Order in Massachusetts.

While the fate of Harvard College was being decided, other developments hastened the emergence of Unitarianism as a distinct religious body. In the early 1800's a new generation of ministers, both liberal and conservative, came to Boston. Most famous among them was William Ellery Channing, who was called to the pulpit of the Federal Street Church. Channing, reluctantly, would become the leader of the liberal clergy in the city.

In addition to new voices from the pulpit, the early years of the century saw new voices in print. A club of young liberals began publishing THE MONTHLY ANTHOLOGY in 1804. This, the first literary magazine in America, was not intended to be theological in its focus, but the sympathies of its publishers resulted in the publication of several articles supportive of the Unitarian cause in the early years of the Unitarian Controversy. A year later, Jedidiah Morse established his own magazine, THE PANOPLIST. For seventeen years it would promote the cause of orthodox Calvinism, and served well to inflame the controversy within the churches. In 1805 a self-educated Universalist clergyman, Hosea Ballou, published A TREATISE ON ATONEMENT, a book-length statement of Universalist theology in which the author clearly and deliberately denied the Doctrine of the Trinity. While its folksy style probably resulted in its having little influence among Unitarians, it succeeded in transforming the emerging Universalists from a trinitarian to a unitarian position within ten years of its publication.

Nor were the Universalists the only group to question the Doctrine of the Trinity. The Quakers split over the issue and the question of liberty of belief, the liberal Hicksites emerging from the main body. The churches of the Christian Connection were frequently unsound on this doctrine. Presbyterian dissidents in the western and border-states were flirting with the Unitarian heresy.

In Massachusetts, despite the struggle over Harvard, there still had been no formal separation of the two parties but the gulf between them continued to grow. It became apparent in 1807, in Deerfield, when orthodox ministers refused to ordain Samuel Willard because in their judgement he did not believe in the Divinity of Christ. At the request of the church that had called Willard to their pulpit, liberal ministers from the eastern part of the state agreed to ordain him. This growing division found additional expression in the refusal of orthodox ministers to exchange pulpits with their liberal colleagues.[32] In 1809, Dr. Morse established Park Street Church in Boston. Located at "Brimstone Corner" this Church was intended to be, and became the Cathedral of Orthodox Congregationalism in Boston, a challenge and a source of irritation to the more liberal clergy of that city.

With these increasing divisions and schisms within congregations and among the clergy, Morse was coming ever closer to his dream of forcing the liberals to declare themselves. Only the right incident was needed to force the conflict into the open. But the liberals would not accommodate him. They steadfastly insisted that they were not Unitarians. Most of them were, in fact, Arian in their theology, but they preferred to avoid controversy about dogma. They defined religion in terms of ethical living, and preferred to call themselves "liberal Christians" or "rational Christians" or "catholic Christians," and called upon their opponents to be open and tolerant.

In 1815 Morse finally found the lever he had been seeking. In

1812 Thomas Belsham of the Essex Street Chapel in London had published a work entitled THE MEMOIRS OF THEOPHILUS LINDSEY. One chapter of that book was devoted to a description of Unitarianism in New England, clearly counting the liberal Congregationalists as Unitarian. When Morse discovered this book, he reprinted that chapter as a pamphlet entitled AMERICAN UNITARIANISM. Then, he reviewed his own pamphlet in THE PANOPLIST. In the review he made three strong points: that the liberals in Massachusetts were, in fact, Unitarians; that they had deliberately concealed that fact in order to spread their beliefs secretly; and therefore orthodox believers ought to separate themselves from the liberals.

The liberals, stung by the charge that they had deliberately concealed their true convictions in order to deceive the public, were finally drawn to answer Morse. As leader of the liberal clergy, William Ellery Channing was chosen to reply. His vehicle was a public letter, in which we argued that most of the liberal clergy were not Unitarian in Belsham's sense, holding to the simple humanity of Jesus, but that they were Arians, granting Christ an exalted place. Further, he insisted that the liberals' views on the Trinity were well known and that they had not preached on the subject because such preaching is disruptive and not conducive to right living. Finally, he deplored Morse's invitation to split apart the Church over a doctrine that is difficult to understand, that defies reason and that has no basis in scripture. Channing ended with an appeal for tolerance and forbearance on all sides.

Samuel Worcester of Salem answered Channing's letter. Thus began a printed debate that would soon shift from the question of whether the liberals were Unitarians to a debate about Unitarianism. In the process the liberals and the orthodox were confirmed more strongly than ever in their respective positions. With those positions sharply defined, ministers and congregations found themselves increasingly required to choose between the contending forces.

At the end of the debate, the liberals discovered that the Unitarian label had been fixed to them permanently and they set about to make the best of it, redefining and expanding its meaning.

Increasingly this doctrinal difference found expression in the life of the local churches. Where they predominated, conservatives resurrected old creeds or drafted new ones, and examined candidates for ordination with great care to determine the orthodoxy of their opinions. When churches sought new ministers for vacant pulpits, often there was controversy over whether the candidate should be from Harvard or Andover. Sometimes, now, the debate spilled over into the sermons preached from the pulpit, and frequently found expression in the annual Convention sermons. An effort to impose a doctrinal test for membership in the Massachusetts Ministers Convention was only narrowly averted.

The controversy, which had forced the liberals into public awareness as a party, and which had attached a label to them, failed to weaken them as Morse had hoped. Rather, it was the occasion for increased efforts among them to work together in a common cause. To meet the competition from Andover, and to ensure a supply of well-qualified ministers, they strengthened the instruction in Divinity at Harvard. Echoes of the controversy were heard beyond the New England region, resulting in the establishment of Unitarian congregations in several major cities. Even Dr. Morse was not safe from the liberal tide. In 1816, a group of members of his Charlestown congregation withdrew and established a Unitarian church. Three years later, those who had remained under his leadership forced Morse's resignation from the pulpit and from the ministry. It is one of the ironies of history that his son, Samuel F. B. Morse, inventor of the telegraph, became a supporter of a radical Unitarianism in his later years.

In 1819, William Ellery Channing was invited to preach the ordination sermon for Jared Sparks, who had been chosen unanimously as the first minister of the newly gathered First Independent Church of Baltimore, Maryland. Having been silent in face of orthodox criticism since his open letter in response to Morse's charges in THE PANOPLIST, Channing determined to use this occasion to respond to his critics and to define and defend his faith. The sermon, entitled UNITARIAN CHRISTIANITY, lasted for an hour and a half. He argued forcefully that the Christianity of the scriptures, when interpreted by reason and conscience, is, in fact, Unitarian. He carefully defined the areas in which orthodox and Unitarians disagreed and subjected the orthodox positions to sweeping and devastating attack. He concluded by urging his listeners:

> Do not, brethren, shrink from the duty of searching God's Word for yourselves, through fear of human censure and denunciation. Do not think, that you may innocently follow the opinions which prevail around you, without investigation, on the ground, that Christianity is now so purified from errors as it need no laborious research. Much stubble is yet to be burned; much rubbish to be removed; many gaudy decorations, which a false taste has hung around Christianity, must be swept away; and the earth-born fogs, which have shrouded it, must be scattered, before this divine fabric will rise before us in its native and awful majesty, in its harmonious proportions, in its mild and celestial splendors.[33]

It has been said that no one seated past the first few rows in the church that day could hear anything Channing said. Whether that be true or not, Channing's Baltimore Sermon was one of the most significant sermons ever preached in the United States. It provided the new movement a center around which to rally its energies, and a powerful propaganda tool. Rushed into print as a pamphlet it went through eight editions in four months. Few sermons in the history of the United States have been as widely read.

The sentiments Channing expressed in Baltimore in May of 1819 struck a chord in a number of places. Four months after the Baltimore Sermon, Jared Sparks preached an ordination sermon for

Samuel Gilman in the new Unitarian church in Charleston, South Carolina. En route to and from this preaching engagement, he preached to Unitarians in Raleigh, North Carolina. In 1821, Sparks founded THE UNITARIAN MISCELLANEY, as a vehicle for spreading the message. That year he was chosen to serve as Chaplain of the U. S. House of Representatives. While in Washington, he preached to a small congregation of Unitarians that had just been organized in the nation's capitol. That same year, 1821, saw the founding of a new church in New York City, the result of the preaching of Henry Ware Jr. who stopped off in New York on his way to and from a preaching engagement in Baltimore.

Nor was the attractiveness of the Unitarian message limited to urban centers on the East Coast. Sparks received communication from nascent Unitarians among the Baptists, Methodists, Presbyterians, and Christians on the frontier beyond the mountains. Unfortunately, the Unitarian movement, centered in eastern Massachusetts, had neither the energy, the organization nor, it must be confessed, sufficient interest to serve those remote groups.

With Channing's sermon receiving so much attention, it was not possible for the evangelical camp to allow it to stand unanswered. Moses Stuart and Leonard Woods of Andover undertook to respond. Channing had nothing to add to what he had said in Baltimore, but Andrews Norton and Henry Ware of Harvard entered the lists on the Unitarian side. Eventually a protracted debate between Woods and Ware (called the Wood'n Ware Controversy) was carried on in print. The argument that had begun in a discussion of scripture soon moved to a focus on reason and conscience and human experience as religious authority. What is more, the Arianism that had been the consensus among the liberals of Channing's generation had begun to evolve into a far more clearly Unitarian position. There would be no way to bridge the spiritual division that had opened between the evangelicals and the liberals in the Congregational Churches in New England.

This spiritual division was widened and deepened by an inevitable contest between the two camps for ownership of church property—a contest that occasioned an important legal case. Complicating the decision process was the fact that in Massachusetts towns there were two distinct, but inter-related religious organizations. The Parish consisted of all the male voters of the town, who supported the church with their taxes. The Church, usually a small minority of the Parish, consisted of those who had made a public profession of faith and who had chosen to join the church. The custom had been that when it was necessary to hire a new minister, the Church would recommend a candidate, and the Parish, in a pro-forma manner, would ratify the recommendation and hire the minister. This customary practice was disrupted, in many places, as a consequence of the division within the Congregational Churches. Sometimes the church was liberal and the parish conservative; more often the parish was liberal and the church conservative. In either case, the result was division, with each side claiming to be the church with legal right to the property and the power to settle the minister of its choice.

The legal battle came to head in 1818 when the church in Dedham found it necessary to choose a new minister. In this case the Parish was liberal while the church was orthodox. The church voted 18-14 to reject a Harvard graduate who, defying custom, had been chosen already by two-thirds of the parish. The majority of the church withdrew from the parish, taking the church's property, and formed a new church. The minority remained with the parish, reorganized, and sued for recovery of the church property.

The Court, after careful consideration, ruled in 1820 that "where a majority of the members of a Congregational Church separate from a majority of the Parish, the members who remain, though a minority, constitute the Church in such Parish, and retain the rights and property belonging thereto."[34] Those who withdrew, according to the Dedham Case, lost all claim on the property of the church.

The decision was an unexpected blow to the evangelical cause. It was not lost on the evangelicals that the judge who issued the ruling was, himself, a Unitarian. Convinced that he had allowed his personal allegiance to influence his decision, they protested in the strongest manner this seizure of property they knew to be theirs. Nonetheless the decision stood. Over the next few years at least 81 "exiled" churches would give up their property. Some 3,900 church members would withdraw from parishes, leaving property valued at $234,000 and funds amounting to $366,000 in the hands of the 1,282 church members who remained with the parishes. The Unitarians were the beneficiaries in most of these cases.[35]

It should also be noted, however, that in other places churches became Unitarian without controversy, some so quietly and insensibly that it becomes impossible to attribute a date to the conversion. In any case, of the 544 Congregational Churches in Massachusetts, 135 became Unitarian. Of the 25 oldest churches in the state, twenty became Unitarian. Only one of the Boston churches remained outside the Unitarian fold. Perhaps more important for the future of the movement, the Unitarians were, for the most part, well educated, financially well-off, theologically liberal, but politically and socially conservative. As a class, they dominated the Supreme Court and the State Government of Massachusetts.

The question confronting the liberals, after the Baltimore Sermon and the Dedham Case, concerned whether they ought to organize a new denomination. At the moment, they were an aggregation of ministers and congregations defined largely by their opponents. The older ministers, always fearful of the consequences of sectarianism, were reluctant to establish a new denomination. They had come this far without sectarian institutions and they preferred to simply allow events to take their natural course. Younger ministers, sensing an opportunity, were eager to organize in order to spread their faith more effectively. For a while, the older ministers prevailed. Being socially and politically conservative they had little interest in seeking converts. They were much more concerned with issues of moral character, civic virtue, public welfare and philanthropy than with spreading Unitarianism to the masses. Indeed, many of them identified with Unitarianism more for the freedom it offered than because of specific doctrines. Thus, many of the older ministers, including Channing, remained reluctant to use the Unitarian label.

Given this state of mind, it is not surprising that denominational structures were slow to develop. The first step had been taken as early as 1820, when a group of ministers, meeting in the vestry of the Federal Street Church organized the Berry Street Conference. The purpose of the conference was to provide mutual support, and to engage in religious publication.[36] The following year the publishing aim of the conference was assumed by the Publishing Fund Society. In 1824, at a meeting of the Anonymous Association, a club of thirty to forty Boston Unitarians, a proposal was presented to advance Unitarianism through an organization devoted to the publication of tracts. Discussion of the proposal was carried on for several months. In May of 1825, at the next meeting of the Berry Street Conference, it was unanimously decided to organize the American Unitarian Association. A committee drafted a constitution and on May 26, 1825—the very day that the British and Foreign Unitarian Association was founded in England—the American Unitarian Association came into being.

This was still far from a denominational structure in the modern sense of the world. The AUA was comprised not of churches but of individual members. Its stated purpose was not to serve congregations or even to co-ordinate their activities, but to spread the word through print. It was poorly funded and received only lukewarm support in many quarters. Nonetheless, it set about its work. It provided a minister to edit THE CHRISTIAN REGISTER, which eventually became the publication of the AUA. In 1827, Dr. Joseph Tuckerman was hired to work as minister at large with the poor of

Boston, work which was assumed by the Benevolent Fraternity of Churches in Boston in 1834. The AUA undertook to explore the potential for churches west of the thirteen original colonies and extended financial aid to churches in Pennsylvania and Georgia. In 1827, the Unitarian Sunday School Society was founded by teachers connected with Unitarian congregations in the Boston area, for the purpose of publishing and distributing text books and Sunday-school papers.

Slowly the AUA began to develop into a useful instrument for spreading the Unitarian gospel. It is quite likely that the development would have been even more gradual were it not for the gathering Calvinist reaction. In 1823, Lyman Beecher was invited to offer a series of special services at the Park Street Church. So effective was Beecher that his preaching sparked a revival among the evangelicals of the area. Some members of Unitarian Churches were drawn to embrace his Calvinist theology, thus goading the Unitarians out of their complacency. Three years later, Beecher would move to Boston and become the minister of the new Hanover Street Church. Beecher challenged Unitarianism directly and became the leader of the orthodox cause.

The new attacks on Unitarianism came from a different direction. In the early years of the Unitarian Controversy the issue had been centered upon the truth or falsehood of the doctrines taught by the liberals. Now the attack focused upon the consequences of Unitarian theology. Orthodox leaders charged that Unitarianism was lukewarm to religion, to morality, to piety, that Unitarians catered to fashionable society, and that as a consequence of Unitarian dominance vice and crime had increased in Boston and moral values were in decline.

Once more it fell to Channing to defend the Unitarians against these charges. At the dedication of Second Unitarian Church in New York in 1826, he addressed the topic, "Unitarian Christianity Most Favorable to Piety." He contrasted the teachings of Unitarianism and orthodoxy, arguing forcefully that Unitarianism was not only the more reasonable, but also the more moral of the alternatives. He likened Calvary to setting up a gallows at the center of history and challenged the moral authority of a theology that demanded the public execution of an innocent man in order to achieve human salvation.

The Unitarians rejoiced in the sermon; the orthodox were outraged. Seeking yet another weak point for attack, the orthodox now charged that Unitarians, while a minority in the state, had managed by dubious means to obtain control of the political structures of the state. Once more it was Channing who responded in behalf of the Unitarians. Eventually, this controversy would result in amending the Constitution of the Commonwealth of Massachusetts in 1834, to provide for the separation of church and state, and the final disestablishment of religion. Unitarians, who opposed this action, were identified as "antidisestablishmentarians." A variety of religious groups, including the Universalists, conbined their efforts and succeeded in ending tax support of all churches. Many evangelical churches obviously preferred to lose public money rather than share it with the Unitarians.

Through all these controversies—perhaps because of them— Unitarianism exhibited a steady, slow growth in major towns and cities not only in New England, but south along the coast, and west toward the frontier. One factor that limited growth was a persistent shortage of ministers to serve new churches, especially churches outside of New England. In 1844, in an effort to respond to this need, a new theological school was established to prepare ministers to serve the churches in the west. Meadville, Pennsylvania, was the site chosen for Meadville Theological School, a joint venture with the Churches of the Christian Connection, a loose association of churches somewhat more conservative than New England Unitarians, but anti-trinitarian in belief, accepting only the Bible as authority. Over the years, the school would prosper, eventually moving to Chicago and merging with a Universalist school to become Meadville Lombard Theological School.

THE TRANSCENDENTALIST CHALLENGE

Having established a separate identity for itself, and having created the beginnings, at least, of institutional structures, Unitarians now found themselves challenged to explore and develop the implications of their faith. Thus far, Unitarianism had distinguished itself by challenging some Calvinist Doctrines. It had discarded the Doctrine of the Trinity, and some had embraced the full humanity of Jesus. Most questioned the strict predestinarianism taught by Calvinism, and the doctrine of original sin. However, Unitarianism, while embracing the need for reason as the tool for interpreting scripture, still rested firmly on scripture as its authority. Indeed, the rationalism upon which Unitarianism relied was the empiricism of Lockean philosophy. Locke had taught that all knowledge depends on the evidence of the senses, that the human being comes into the world a blank slate, on which the senses write. There can be no reliable knowledge that does not derive directly or indirectly from the senses.

When that assumption was applied to religious truth, a curious logic resulted. If all knowledge must be based on sensory evidence, then religious truth must also have a sensory base. The sensory base upon which Christianity is established can be found in the scriptures, which report the experience of the witnesses and thus comprise the indirect evidence, the written record of the direct sensory experiences of the first Christians. The truth of Christianity depends upon the trustworthiness of that witness. Therefore, the history recounted in the scriptures, including the miracles and the supernatural events that are recorded in the scriptures, must be historically true, for if they are not, then Christianity has no reliable foundation. To a degree greater even than the orthodox, Unitarians defended the truth of the scripture because it offered the only reliable basis for religious truth. Much of Unitarian thought and teaching and many Unitarian sermons were devoted to detailed, scholarly attempts to prove and defend the truth of the scriptures.

John Locke's philosophy, however, was not without its challengers. Jonathan Edwards had suggested that the mind must be endowed with an innate structure or process of knowing which allows it to order and sort and comprehend the data provided by the senses. This inherent structure underlies all meaning and comprehension. In Germany, Kant, Fichte, Schleiermacher and others had begun to challenge the notion that all knowledge derives from the senses. They seemed to be suggesting that human beings have direct access to truth, to a reality that transcends the testimony of the senses. This new philosophy was transmitted to the English speaking world through the English Romantics, Coleridge, Carlyle, Wordsworth, and others.[37]

The implication for religion of a new understanding concerning the foundations of knowledge, at first, was a matter of scholarly dialogue. But ultimately, the conversation would move out into the wider community, and drift into a more public venue, particularly among the educated classes from which Unitarians drew their support. By 1836, a group known as the Transcendental Club was meeting irregularly to discuss the new philosophy, popularly known as Transcendentalism. Inevitably, the insights of this new understanding began to be voiced in public lectures and even in sermons but without provoking any public expressions of apprehension or concern.

The circumstance that would make Transcendentalism an issue within Unitarianism arose in the summer of 1838, when the students of Harvard Divinity School invited Ralph Waldo Emerson to address the graduating class. Emerson had served as minister of Second Church in Boston for three years, but had resigned, in part because of his discomfort with the rite of communion. He left the active ministry and devoted himself to literature and the lecture hall.

On July 15, 1838, Emerson delivered his ground-breaking DI-
VINITY SCHOOL ADDRESS. He took this occasion to voice his dissatisfaction with the "corpse cold Unitarianism" of his day. He criti-
cized Unitarian ministers who devoted their sermons to dry and
arid disquisitions focused on the recorded experiences of men long
dead, while ignoring their own first-hand experience of life. He described the preacher who tempted him never again to go to church:

A snow storm was falling around us. The snow storm
was real, the preacher merely spectral; and the eye felt the
sad contrast in looking at him, and then at the window behind him, into the beautiful meteor of the snow. He had lived
in vain. He had not one word intimating that he had laughed
or wept, was married or in love, had been commended or
cheated or chagrined. If he had ever lived and acted, we were
none the wiser for it. The capital secret of his profession,
namely, to convert life into truth, he had not learned. Not
one fact in all his experience, had he yet imported into his
doctrine. This man had ploughed, and planted, and talked,
and bought, and sold; he had read books; he had eaten and
drunken; his head aches; his heart throbs; he smiles and suf-
fers; yet was there not a surmise, a hint, in all the discourse
that he had ever lived at all. Not a line did he draw out of
real history. The true preacher can be known by this, that he
deals out to the people his life—life passed through the fire
of thought.[38]

The speaker went on to urge his listeners to abandon the traditional focus on the testimony of the past as the source of religious
truth, and to focus instead upon their own lives, their own experience of the sacred. He insisted that God not only spoke in the past,
but speaks today to those who open themselves to the meaning of
their experience of the world. He insisted that:

The stationariness of religion; the assumption that the
age of inspiration is past, that the Bible is closed; the fear of

degrading the character of Jesus by representing him as a man; indicate with sufficient clearness the falsehood of our theology. It is the office of a true teacher to show us that God is, not was; that He speaketh, not spake. . . .Yourself a new-born bard of the Holy Ghost,—cast behind you all conformity, and acquaint men at first hand with deity.[39]

The response to Emerson's address was swift, and for the most part hostile. Newspapers, ministers, and professors all hastened to distance themselves from his sentiments. The students were warned that it would be damaging to their careers to take Emerson seriously. Emerson's successor at Second Church pointed out that Emerson was not representative of the denomination, and that he was no longer a regular minister. The CHRISTIAN EXAMINER, in a review of the speech insisted that the address was "neither good divinity nor good sense," while Andrews Norton of Harvard, addressing the alumni of the Divinity School called Emerson's views, "the latest form of infidelity."[40]

Norton went on in his address to the alumni to suggest that the miracles reported in the New Testament constitute the foundation of Christianity and that anyone who could not accept the importance of the scriptural witness and the miracles to which it attested had no claim upon the Christian name, and certainly should not be accounted a minister. Emerson refused to make any reply to his critics, but a number of the younger ministers in Boston, among them George Ripley, Theodore Parker and Richard Hildreth wrote anonymous responses and engaged Norton in a modest debate.

The effect of the Divinity School Address was to challenge in public the ancient assumptions concerning the supernatural origins of Christianity and the reliability of the testimony on which it is founded. From this moment on, ministers would be required to decide how they stood in relation to Emerson, since they could assume the question would be asked when a church was seeking a new minister.

Before the controversy could fully run its course, another occasion presented itself, which renewed the excitement. Charles Shackford was called to be minister of the Hawes Place Church in south Boston, and invited Theodore Parker to preach his ordination sermon. Parker was one of the students who had been in the audience to hear Emerson's Divinity School Address. The son of a poor farmer, Parker had become minister of a country church at West Roxbury. He was widely respected for his skills as a parish minister, his broad knowledge, and his deep scholarship, though he was suspected, in some quarters as being one of the Transcendentalists.

Parker chose as the subject for his sermon, THE TRANSIENT AND THE PERMANENT IN CHRISTIANITY. If Emerson had undermined the supernatural basis of Christianity, Parker took the argument to a new level. He suggested that Christianity could not be validated by miracles or by scriptural witnesses or even by the authority of Jesus. Rather, he suggested that if Christianity is true, its truth must be axiomatic and self-evident, and would be just as true if Jesus had never existed, or if the message had been proclaimed in Athens rather than in Palestine. The forms and the doctrines of Christianity, he insisted, are all transient. What is permanent is the word of God expressed in each human heart, the word of God spoken through Conscience, Reason, and Faith and that truth existed before Jesus, and after him and in all times and places.

Christianity does not rest on the infallible authority of the New Testament. It depends on this collection of books for the historical statement of its facts. In this we do not require infallible inspiration on the part of the writers, more than in the record of other historical facts....I cannot see that it depends on the personal authority of Jesus. He was the organ through which the Infinite spoke....So if it could be proved,—as it cannot,—in opposition to the greatest amount of historical evidence ever collected on any similar point, that the gospels were the fabrication of designing and artful

men, that Jesus of Nazareth had never lived, still Christianity would stand firm, and fear no evil....If Christianity were
true, we should still think it was so, not because its record
was written by infallible pens; nor because it was lived out
by an infallible teacher,—but that it is true, like the axioms
of geometry, because it is true, and is to be tried by the oracle
God places in the breast. If it rest on the personal authority
of Jesus alone, then there is no certainty of its truth....[41]

Parker made clear and unmistakable the implication of
Emerson's thought. Christianity was to be seen as one expression of
eternal truth; that same truth found expression in other religions
and was rooted in the human soul. The Christian claim to unique-
ness could no longer be sustained. What is more, he delivered his
message in language that was clear beyond question—so clear, in
fact, that some felt he had treated the most ancient virtues and values with irreverence. Many in the audience were hurt and shocked
by what they had heard. Even so, the matter might have passed
without much consequence were it not for the fact that several orthodox ministers in the audience took notes, and published their
review of what Parker had said, asking, in effect, whether the minister of the Roxbury Church represented the thinking of the denomination. They suggested that in all fairness, Unitarians should either
disown the heresy preached by Mr. Parker, or else make public confession that he represented the true position of the Unitarian denomination.

Stung by the suggestion that Parker's views were normative in
the denomination, and eager to distance themselves from such heresy, many Unitarians were quick to cast Parker beyond the pale.
Some ministers, calling him an unbeliever and an atheist, refused to
speak to him, to shake his hand, or sit beside him in meetings. Most
of the Boston ministers refused to exchange pulpits with him. Many,
including his friend, Channing, doubted that he could be considered Christian any longer. The Boston Association of Congregational

Ministers, to which Parker belonged, considered ejecting him, and finding that unacceptable, sought to have him withdraw voluntarily. Parker, however, refused to resign. In truth, he remained an embarrassment for Unitarianism, since, under Congregational Polity, there was no way to remove him from the ministry so long as his own congregation was satisfied with him. After 1846, the Unitarian Year Book never listed his name among the ministers of the denomination, and the Boston Association, from which he refused to resign, never listed him as a member.

It should not be assumed, however, that Parker was without supporters. A handful of ministers continued to exchange pulpits with him, though never without controversy in their own congregations. When it became clear that most the city's pulpits were closed to him, a group of Boston laymen determined that Mr. Parker should be heard in their community. They hired a hall and arranged for him to preach. A large congregation was gathered and organized in 1846 as the Twenty-eighth Congregational Society, with Parker as its settled minister. So large were the crowds coming to hear him preach on the topics of the day that it soon became necessary to find a larger hall. For years Parker, rejected by most of his own denomination, would be the most popular, the most influential Preacher in Boston and his influence would extend beyond the confines of the city to touch the mind of Abraham Lincoln.[42]

In addition to his ministry, Parker threw himself into the social reforms that defined his day. He grew steadily more radical as he became active in the temperance movement, in the movement for prison reform and opposition to capital punishment, in his concern over slavery and women's rights, in his opposition to war. In time, Parker would write his sermons with a loaded pistol on his desk, ready to defend the runaway slaves he was harboring, and would denounce the Constitution of the United States as a pact with the devil because it countenanced slavery.

After years of lonely, intense labor, Parker's health broke. He undertook a European trip in hope that rest and new vistas might restore his vigor. In 1860, Parker died while in Florence, and was buried in the English Cemetery there. In time, this man who had been an embarrassment to colleagues in his own generation, and who had been an outcast in his own time, would be seen as a great Unitarian prophet, second only to Channing in his influence and importance in the development of the denomination.[43]

Unitarianism had begun as a mild revision of an arcane theological dogma. It had moved gradually from an Arianism which thought Jesus to be less than God, but exalted over all other beings, to a Unitarianism which saw Jesus as the chosen prophet of God, fully human, but exalted above all other Prophets of God. This Unitarianism embraced the miracles and supernatural events that characterized his life and ministry as necessary evidence of God's election of Jesus as his spokesman. Emerson and Parker were not content to allow Unitarianism to rest on this doctrinal plateau. They were seeking a religion more immediate, more personal, more experiential. They were seeking a religion which was not dependent upon the accuracy of the historical record, but which grew out of a deep, internal sense of the sacred and holy dimension of existence.

The consequence of this line of reasoning was to challenge the very foundations of Christian Unitarianism. After Parker and Emerson, it would no longer be possible to assume that everyone understood what Christianity is, or who is entitled to the name, Christian. In the wake of their challenge, Unitarianism found it increasingly necessary to define the relationship of their movement to the great body of Christianity. The effort to undertake that definition, known as the "Radical Controversy," would trouble the denomination for the better part of twenty years, until the Civil War consumed the nation's energies and attentions.

The influence of Transcendentalism, of course, was not confined to Unitarianism. The Transcendentalists were identified with what has been called "the flowering of New England," the great literary movement which included Emerson, Thoreau, the Alcotts, the Longfellows, Dickinson, Melville, et al. through which Unitarian Transcendentalism was mediated to a larger audience. The Transcendentalists were responsible for Dial Magazine, edited by Margaret Fuller, for introducing modern criticism of the Bible, and for engendering in a larger public a new religious sense that sought truth not in the past, nor in supernatural events, but in nature and in the personal response to the natural world.

This emerging religious sense inevitably found expression from the pulpit, as the new teaching made its way into colleges and divinity schools and as younger ministers, having grown up in this atmosphere, sought to give expression to their own deepest religious sensibilities. Among older and more conservative ministers there was a growing alarm at the "excessive radicalism and irreverence of some 'who show no respect to the Scriptures and deny the supernatural in the history of Christianity and in the life of its founder.'"[44] The conservative leaders felt that the slow growth of the movement could be explained by the presence among them of ministers who had abandoned the foundations of Christianity and they felt increasing compulsion to disassociate the movement from such opinions.

However, given the structures of Congregational polity, there was no mechanism for disciplining or restraining unorthodox opinion. The American Unitarian Association was an organization of individuals, not of churches, and as such, could speak for itself but not for anyone else. In 1853, the AUA did what it could do. It adopted a resolution that stated:

Resolved, That the divine authority of the Gospel, as founded on a special and miraculous interposition of God for the redemption of mankind, is the basis of the action of this association.[45]

This resolution, adopted unanimously, and confirmed by similar action by the Western Unitarian Conference, was as close to a creed as history and polity would allow. However, if its purpose was to re-invigorate the movement, it fell far short of that goal. The "radicals" in the movement were offended by a statement that seemed designed not to respond to their concerns but rather to avoid giving offense to the orthodox Christians. Indeed, when a proposal was made to erect a monument to Servetus to observe the three hundredth anniversary of his death, it was opposed by those who feared that "it would offend the orthodox." With good reason did James Freeman Clark call the Unitarians a "discouraged denomination"[46]

Despite the opposition of the majority of the clergy, Theodore Parker's views continued to gain support among some of the younger and more able clergy, whose potential contribution to the movement was frequently thwarted by the hostility of their colleagues. Gradually support for the American Unitarian Association dwindled, which resulted in less aid available for new and marginal churches, many of which withered and died. Nonetheless, the AUA struggled on, raising a fund in 1854 for publication of books, and that same year, appointing C. H. A. Dall as missionary in India, where he planted several churches and schools.

Fortunately, the future of the movement did not rest wholly with the American Unitarian Association, or with its conservative clergy. The great western migration had begun and among those taking the long journey west were Unitarians from New England. Many of them took their religious heritage with them. As they settled the frontier, they sought to establish churches that would reflect that heritage. Thus, the first church erected in Kansas and the first minister in the territory were Unitarian. Milwaukee, San Francisco, Detroit and a large number of other places were claimed for Unitarianism. Only in the south did the movement fail to expand significantly. It was in this period that Meadville Theological School was established, sending a steady supply of ministers into the western regions. And in 1852, the Western Unitarian Association was founded to create and service new churches west of the mountains. In 1855, a missionary to the Chippewa Indians in Minnesota was appointed.

All in all, despite controversy and the continuing attacks of the orthodox and the expenditure of energies upon a number of social causes, including abolition, women's rights, prison reform, mental hospital reform, child labor reform, Unitarianism in 1860 was substantially stronger than it had been at the beginning of the Radical Controversy in the 1840's. However, growth and extension ceased as the nation confronted the horror of Civil War.

The years leading up to the Civil War found the Unitarians, like much of the nation, unable to speak with one voice on the great controversy tearing the country apart. An unknown number of Unitarians were part of the Underground Railroad which aided escaping slaves fleeing from slavery to freedom in Canada. Radicals, like Theodore Parker, and other abolitionists, like Rev. Samuel J. May of Syracuse, New York, opposed fugitive slave laws and urged civil disobedience in response to immoral and unjust laws. Indeed, Parker was among the supporters of John Brown's raid on the arsenal at Harper's Ferry, Virginia. On the other hand many of the socially conservative Unitarians were fearful of the consequences for social order and stability if radical abolitionists were allowed to disrupt the compromises by which the nation had structured a precarious peace.

Once it became clear that Civil War could not be avoided, Unitarians threw themselves into the effort to win the great struggle. Sixty Unitarian ministers entered the Union army. A Unitarian minister, Henry Whitney Bellows, headed the U.S. Sanitary Commission, charged with meeting the needs of sick and wounded soldiers. He was strongly aided and abetted in his task by Mary Livermore, a Universalist and wife of a Universalist minister. William G. Eliot, minister of the First Unitarian Church of St. Louis served as leader of the Western Sanitary Commission. Thomas Wentworth

Higginson, another Unitarian minister, commanded a black regiment in the Union Army. Thomas Starr King, raised a Universalist and now minister of First Unitarian Church of San Francisco, tramped back and forth across California, pleading the Union cause, raising money for the Sanitary Commission, and undermining his health and shortening his life in the process. Starr King is credited with saving California for the Union. And, of course, unnumbered Unitarians served in the Union army.

ORGANIZING A NATIONAL MOVEMENT

When the war ended in 1865, Unitarians, like many others, discovered that they had been profoundly changed by the experience. The regionalism that had characterized the country before the war had been burned away in the great national conflagration. In its place was a new sense of nationhood, one that called for a national institutional response in place of the ad hoc, parochial structures to which the movement had been accustomed. In December of 1864, Bellows, drawing on his experience with the Sanitary Commission, proposed a similar organization for the support and advancement of liberal religion.

An invitation was extended to each church to send its minister and two delegates to a convention to meet in New York City to organize a national convention. Over two hundred churches were represented at this meeting—the first time that Unitarian churches were directly represented in such a general organization. The purpose of the meeting was to create the National Conference of Unitarian Churches.

Knowing that the conflict between the Radical and the Conservative factions had been postponed, but not resolved during years when the nation was consumed by Civil War, the leadership of the convention attempted to find a middle ground between the two poles of opinion. On the first day, it was clear that the conflict could not be avoided for long. A leading layman proposed a series of resolutions that would have committed the new organization to a conservative creed. The proposal was tabled and not brought up again for consideration. It was agreed, however, that decisions by the body would be understood to be the opinion of those at the meeting, and not binding on the conscience of any individual. The leadership then proceeded to limit debate and to present the articles of the proposed constitution for consideration, leaving aside the preamble until the end. Having approved the articles of the constitution, the meeting went on to deal with a number of practical matters. It approved raising $100,000 for denominational purposes and a similar fund for Antioch College in Ohio. As a result of this effort, churches were founded in Ann Arbor, Michigan; Ithaca, New York; and a number of other college towns, and missionaries were sent south to revive churches that had been closed during the war, and to California to establish new churches. In addition, the Convention proposed union with the Universalists, and urged the creation of a new denominational publication

However, when the preamble for the new constitution was presented the radicals, who had hoped for a broadly inclusive church, were profoundly disappointed. The preamble affirmed that Unitarians were "'disciples of the Lord Jesus Christ' and devoted 'to the service of God and the building-up of the kingdom of his son.'"[47] The rules of debate developed by the leadership permitted very little time for expressing views or engaging issues. Ultimately, the preamble was adopted. Despite Bellows' promise that at the next meeting of the Conference the issues raised by the wording of the preamble would be fully discussed, the radicals left the meeting deeply discontented.

For a year, the radical and conservative factions gathered their forces and prepared for the meeting in Syracuse. The radicals proposed amending the preamble of the constitution by deleting the words "disciples of our Lord Jesus Christ." The conservatives insisted that to abandon these words, now that they were already part of the constitution, would be interpreted as rejecting their historic allegiance. The meeting, by a vote of two to one, defeated the proposal, though they did agree to change the name of the conference to read, "National Conference of Unitarian and Independent Churches." The radicals were not mollified. Instead, feeling they had been betrayed, they determined to withdraw from the conference and form a new organization based on freedom of belief.

In May of 1867, after months of informal discussion, a meeting was held in Boston to consider the creation of an organization outside Unitarianism to serve the needs of free religion. At the meeting a constitution was adopted and officers elected, and the Free Religious Association came into being. Its purpose was "to promote the interests of pure religion, to encourage the scientific study of religion and to increase fellowship in the spirit."[48] Although Unitarian ministers represented a large portion of the original membership, most of them never left the Unitarian denomination. Nor did the Free Religious Association seek to establish churches or develop a program. It did, however, publish significant materials and periodicals, and was content to function as a voice for radical religion, and as a separate focus of influence upon the Unitarian movement. The Association held annual meetings well into the twentieth century, although its influence diminished over time as the religious radicals felt increasingly comfortable within the mainstream of Unitarianism.

The National Conference of Unitarian and Independent Churches went about its business, raised the money that had been pledged for the Denomination and for Antioch College, pledged support for Meadville, and supported the organization of new congregations. The year following the creation of the Free Religious Association, aware of the challenge it represented, the National Conference voted to amend its preamble in an effort to ease the consciences of the radicals. The amendment affirmed that the declarations in the constitution, including the preamble, were expressions of the majority, but were not binding upon those who disagreed with them.

Now it was the turn of the conservatives to be affronted. It seemed to them that the radicals had gained all that they had sought; it seemed to them that the divinity schools had become centers of radical thought and that the denomination was on the verge of cutting the ties to its heritage. Unable to move the Convention, they turned to the American Unitarian Association, seeking a statement of faith for the Denomination. Thwarted in this attempt, the conservatives contemplated establishing an Evangelical Unitarian Association. In a circular letter, conservative leaders urged churches to withhold financial support from the national movement.

In 1870 the issue came to the attention of the National Conference once more. After lengthy debate, in which the radicals were hissed, the Conference voted overwhelmingly to reaffirm allegiance to Jesus Christ. And there the issue remained for a dozen years, while the radicals, alienated from the denominational institutions, quietly increased their strength in the churches and schools. Periodically, however, events would conspire to bring the issue back to attention.

One such event would be known as the Year-book Controversy. It had been a long-standing custom for the denomination to publish an annual year-book, which included a list of churches and ministers. In 1873, Octavius Brooks Frothingham, president of the Free Religious Association, indicated surprise that his name should be included in that list since he no longer accepted Jesus as his leader, and requested that the editor remove his name. The Secretary of the Free Religious Association, William Potter, wrote the editor saying that though he was a Unitarian, he was no longer a Christian, allowing the editor to decide whether or not to include his name. The editor decided to drop Potter, and Frothingham, and, without consulting them, a number of other ministers judged to be not Christian. Conservatives approved; radicals were outraged. For ten years the issue of the year-book was debated, and over time it was transformed into an issue of freedom of belief versus creedal restriction. In 1882, the National Conference responded to this concern by adopting a new article for the constitution, which, while affirming that the preamble and articles of the constitution reflected the opinion of the majority of Unitarians, "they are no authoritative test of Unitarianism, and are not intended to exclude from our fellowship any who, while differing from us in belief, are in general sympathy with our purposes and practical aims."[49] Eventually, in 1884, the radical ministers were restored to the list.

While this controversy was troubling the national movement, it found resonance particularly in the Western Unitarian Conference. The Conference had been established in 1852. It was charged with serving the widely scattered churches in the Mississippi basin. Geographically distant from Boston, and older than the National Conference, the Western Unitarian Conference early developed a strong sense of independence. With its own staff and a number of parallel structures, the Western Conference was almost a denomination unto itself.

By 1875, the Western Conference had become more radical than its eastern counterpart. In that year it voted unanimously that "the Western Conference conditions its fellowship on no dogmatic tests, but welcomes all thereto who desire to work with it in advancing the Kingdom of God."[50] At the same time, the Conference sent resolutions of good will both to the Free Religious Association and to the National Conference.

This stance served to alarm conservative Unitarians in the Western Conference. Fearful of growing irreligion, they agitated for a creed that would keep agnostics, materialists and spiritualists out. The issue came to a head in Cincinnati in 1886, when the matter was debated at the annual meeting. On their part, conservatives felt that the welfare of the movement demanded that Unitarians affirm their Christian faith in God, while the radicals argued that Unitarianism was rooted in freedom from creeds of any kind imposed by any authority. The debate was long and heated, but in the end a decisive majority determined that "the Western Unitarian Conference conditions its fellowship on no dogmatic tests, but welcomes all who wish to join it to help establish Truth, Righteousness and Love in the World."[51]

It was a remarkable decision. Not only had the Western Unitarian Conference refused to define itself as Christian, it had refused to make any form of theism a requirement for fellowship. Now agnostics or even, presumably, atheists who shared a concern for the moral and ethical qualities of life were welcome in Unitarianism. The door that Emerson had unlocked and Parker had nudged had been thrown wide open by the Western Conference.

Inevitably, the conservatives withdrew from the Western Unitarian Conference and organized a rival Western Unitarian Association. The National Association refused all support or co-operation with the Western Unitarian Conference and threw its weight behind the Western Unitarian Association. Until 1896, the Issue in the West continued to trouble the denomination with the two rival organizations competing for the loyalty and the support of western Unitarians. In that year, the Western Unitarian Association ceased to exist, and the radical position of the Western Unitarian Conference prevailed.

Beginning in the 1870's a number of developments in the outside world had the cumulative effect of slowing the development of Unitarianism, and forcing the denomination to focus energy and resources upon strengthening existing churches rather than establishing new ones. Thus, the great Chicago fire in 1871 destroyed Robert Collyer's Unitarian Church in that city. The denomination would raise $60,000 to help rebuild it. The following year a fire in Boston's financial district devastated the denomination's finances. These catastrophes were followed by a series of economic panics and depressions that made it increasingly difficult for the denomination to raise funds. Nonetheless, new projects were undertaken and new institutional structures created. In 1880 a national Women's Auxiliary Conference was established. In 1884 churches became members of the American Unitarian Association for the first time and the AUA became a denominational structure rather than an organization of individuals. In 1889 the Conference established a mission in Japan. In 1896 the Young People's Religious Union was established to serve the young people of the movement. By 1900 the denomination had grown to twice the size it had been in 1865 when the National Conference had been established, and it was poised to join in the great movement for social renewal known as the Social Gospel. Harking back to the work of Joseph Tuckerman with the poor of Boston, and to the ancient Unitarian conviction that Christianity should be concerned more with the "religion of Jesus" than with the "religion about Jesus," the Social Gospel seemed to be the ratification of Unitarian concerns by the larger religious community.

FACING A NEW AGE

The great work of the Social Gospel in establishing the "Christian century" was interrupted by the calamity of the First World War, which made a mockery of much of the idealism with which Americans had entered upon the new era. At the outbreak of the war, the American Unitarian Association called upon its churches to support the government and the war effort. In a clear violation of the principle of congregational polity, the Association announced that it would withhold all support from any church whose minister did not wholeheartedly support the war aims of the government. John Haynes Holmes, minister of The Church of the Messiah, in New York, refused to support the war and, after a public confrontation with former President, William Howard Taft, who was presiding over the sessions of the Unitarian Conference which met in Montreal that October, Holmes and his church virtually withdrew from the denomination. Eventually, when the war was over, the AUA apologized for its transgression, and welcomed Homes and his congregation back into fellowship. If nothing else, the incident served as a reminder of how much a part of the national establishment Unitarianism was, and how vulnerable it was to conventional thinking, even at the expense of its ancient principles.

Holmes was a radical influence in the denomination not only because of his pacifism in the face of a nation at war, but also because of his vision of the nature of religion. He called for a religion which was based on "modernism," by which he meant a religion stripped of the miraculous, free of all supernaturalism and based in the natural world. He called for a religion that moved from concentration on the individual and focused instead on the social nature of every individual. Holmes saw religion as a process of social change and the church as the agent of social change. As a consequence, he shifted the basis of religion from concern about God to concern for humanity; he shifted the center of religious life from the individual to the social group; and defined the community as the unit of social integration.

Holmes foreshadowed the great controversy of the early twentieth century—the Humanist Controversy. Among the leaders of the humanist movement within Unitarianism were Curtis W. Reese, John H. Dietrich and Charles Francis Potter. Reese had opened the discussion in 1920 when he addressed the Harvard Summer School of Theology. In his address Reese said:

> Historically, the basic content of religious liberalism is spiritual freedom. Out of this basic content has come the conviction of the supremacy of reason, of the primary worth of character, and of the immediate access of man to spiritual sources. Always religious liberalism has tended to replace alleged divine revelations and commands with human opinions and judgments; to develop the individual attitude in religion; and to identify righteousness with life. The method

of religious liberalism has always been that of reflection, not that of authority. Liberalism has insisted on the essentially natural character of religion....The theology of Augustine and that of Channing, the theology of Billy Sunday and that of H. G. Wells, might all be found utterly inadequate without consequent injury to the religion of the liberal. Liberalism is building a religion that would not be shaken even if the thought of God were out-grown.[52]

The address, which linked religious liberalism to the social and political currents of the day, aroused significant discussion and opposition, for it seemed to cut the last tenuous ties to traditional views of religion. Reese appeared quite prepared to abandon not only the Christian God, but also the very concept of God. Among the outspoken opponents of Reese's views was William L. Sullivan, a former Catholic priest who had become a Unitarian minister. Sullivan undertook to debate the issue with John Dietrich, minister of the church in Minneapolis, and a leading spokesman for religious humanism, at the meeting of the National Conference in 1921, thus introducing the controversy to a larger audience.

The debate continued throughout the decade. In some ways, the controversy within Unitarianism reflected a similar concern in the larger society—one that came to a head in 1926, with the Scopes trial, which seemed to pit naturalism and supernaturalism in a contest for public support. John Dietrich's preaching in his church in Minneapolis became a center for a growing body of religious humanists within the Unitarian movement. In 1933, a group of humanists in Chicago issued the Humanist Manifesto, an attempt to define the values and the convictions of humanists in a clear and concise manner. The Manifesto defined the universe as self-existing, not the work of a creator, saw man as part of nature, rejected revelation as a basis for religion, affirmed science as the basis of all knowledge of the universe and declared theism of any kind to be outdated. The Manifesto was signed among others by a number of

Unitarian ministers, and one Universalist minister.

While the echoes of the humanist-theist controversy would be heard well into the middle of the century, so strong was the humanist influence in the movement that the very basis of theism was shifted. Increasingly among Unitarian theists, the term God came to be used as a convenient symbol for that power beyond human control in which human existence is rooted—in some cases, little more than a poetic personification of the Universe itself, and often used in ways quite compatible with all but the most rigid interpretations of humanism. Ultimately, Unitarian Christians found it necessary to organize a group with the Association, the Unitarian Christian Fellowship, to sustain a Christian witness within Unitarianism.

Although the controversy between humanists and theists demonstrated that there was still intellectual and theological vitality among Unitarians, the early years of the century had not dealt well with the movement. New churches were few during those years, many congregations were dependent for their survival upon financial support from the national body and a number of existing churches had failed altogether. In 1934, an eight member Commission of Appraisal, chaired by Frederick May Eliot, was appointed to evaluate the American Unitarian Association. The report of the Commission, UNITARIANS FACE A NEW AGE, was a stirring call to action. In response to the recommendations of the commission, the AUA introduced a number of structural changes, among them, strengthening the presidency. In addition, Unitarians embraced new approaches to extension work, and theological education. Dr. Eliot, chosen president of the American Unitarian Association in 1937, found himself in a position to pursue the recommendations of the commission with vigor. The result was a period of new growth and dynamism for Unitarianism in America.

In 1937, the Association established the New Beacon Series curriculum for the Religious Education of its children. Under the leadership of Sophia Lyon Fahs, the new Beacon Curriculum took as its focus the experience and the needs of the children rather than the traditional body of religious teaching and understood the method of teaching as religiously significant. A tired and drab religious education program took on new life and vigor.

In 1940, responding to the plight of refugees from the war consuming the ancient states of Europe, the Unitarian Service Committee was created. In the midst of that war, A. Powell Davies, minister of the Unitarian Church in Summit, New Jersey, and the pre-eminent Unitarian preacher of the day, pronounced the five principles of modern Unitarianism:

1. Individual freedom of belief
2. Discipleship to advancing truth
3. Democratic process in human relations
4. Universal brotherhood, undivided by nations, race, or creed
5. Allegiance to the cause of a United World Community.

This, in many ways, was the basis upon which Unitarianism would move into the post-war world. It is a remarkable statement, fully indicative of how far American Unitarianism had traveled on its journey out of the Christian consensus. It is a methodological statement, which avoids all the traditional religious terms—God, Jesus, Christianity, etc. In many ways, it embraces as normative the Humanism preached by Curtis Reese at Harvard in 1920. On the basis of this understanding of Unitarianism, the Fellowship movement, a program for organizing lay-led congregations, was established, and led Unitarianism into a period of dramatic growth and renewal in the decade of the 1950's[53].

Universalism in the United States[54]

Despite the fact that Unitarianism had a long organizational history in Eastern Europe and a substantial development within the British Isles, early Unitarians on the North American Continent were reluctant to claim that history and to be identified with it. Unitarians in New England had preferred to think of themselves as the legitimate heirs of English Puritanism, as liberal, or catholic Christians rather than as the spiritual offspring of acknowledged heretics like Francis David, Faustus Socinus, or John Biddle. They remained suspicious of contemporary English Unitarians like Joseph Priestley and sought to distance themselves from the movement in England. The Unitarian name was forced on them, and accepted by them only with the greatest reluctance.

By contrast, the Universalists, who—except for sporadic and short-lived congregations—had no separate organized existence in Europe before their founding in North America, were quick to search out and to affirm their European roots. Almost from the first, they embraced the universalism of Clement and Origen of Alexandria, and asserted that the majority of earliest Christians had been universalist in their theology, believing in the ultimate salvation of all. They scrabbled about in medieval records to discover evidence that universalism, denounced by the church as a heresy, had retained an underground existence even in that inhospitable era. They were quick to embrace the expressions of universalism which were part of late medieval mysticism. They listed the radical reformers who had affirmed universalism along with their various other heresies. They were determined to demonstrate that the "greater gospel" which they preached was not some recent enthusiasm, but represented the true inner meaning of the Christian gospel.

Universalists were not without substantial justification in this undertaking. The fact is that universalism has maintained a stubborn existence throughout most of the history of the Christian Church. It has been nourished by many of the mystic schools which have emerged from within Christianity. But universalism would not be embodied within a distinct organizational structure until the late eighteenth century, and then, it would emerge in New England.

Universalism in North American has two distinct roots, both nourished in the left wing of European Protestantism. One source of American Universalism can be traced to Pennsylvania around 1719, when an influx of German Brethren—those who would be known as the "Pennsylvania Dutch"—established communities in the south-eastern and south-central part of the colony. These German groups were characterized by a variety of radical opinions. They were anabaptists, rejecting the notion of infant baptism. They were pietists, rejecting involvement with the larger world. They were spiritualists, relying upon the testimony of the Bible as interpreted by the Holy Spirit. Many of them were also universalists, convinced that in the end, all of creation would be restored to harmony with God, and that anything less than universal salvation was unthinkable since that would imply divine failure.

Into this religious community, in 1741 came George de Benneville. De Benneville was the son of religious refugees who had fled their native France to live in England under the protection of the English monarch. As a young man, de Benneville had experienced a mystical vision of heaven, and had come to believe that the true message of the Christian gospel was the ultimate salvation of all. At seventeen, he had traveled to France on missionary journeys to spread the good word, and was twice imprisoned, once escaping execution only because of the intervention of the Queen. After a preaching career in Holland and Germany, he had accepted the invitation of a universalist Quaker, Christopher Sauer, to make a life for himself in the new world.

Settled in Pennsylvania, de Benneville eventually built a home in the Oley valley near modern Reading. He served as physician to settlers and native Americans alike. He found the indigenous peoples a source of great wisdom and insight, and sought to supplement his medical knowledge by learning their techniques and wisdom. However respected he was as a physician, de Benneville was more than a healer of the body. He was also a preacher. In the home he built, he constructed a large room on the second floor where he preached his mystical universalism to all who would listen.

As his reputation grew, his contacts grew as well. He was welcomed as a friend at the Ephrata Cloisters. Established by German Brethren, known as Dunkers, the Cloisters was an intentional, semimonastic community that believed, among other things, in the final restoration of all things. De Benneville's brand of pious, mystical universalism was widely accepted in this religious community, and it must be assumed that when, in 1744, missionaries from Ephrata undertook journeys to the shores of Barnegat Bay in New Jersey, the gospel they preached included this universalism.

De Benneville did not rely on the spoken word and the efforts of preachers and missionaries only, to spread the universalist gospel. His friend, Christopher Sauer, had established a press and had published a number of universalist texts, among them, THE EVERLASTING GOSPEL by Georg Klein-Nicolai of Friessdorf, a book which would influence the first generation of Universalists. De Benneville also collaborated in the publication of the Sauer Bible, a German language Bible in which the traditional texts supporting universalism were printed in boldface type.

Late in his life, de Benneville moved to Philadelphia, where he died. His direct influence on Universalism is difficult to trace. He established no churches; his work was largely with religious communities which affirmed universalism, but for whom that affirmation was not the defining center of their faith. When he died, he left no continuing institutions, but there can be little doubt that he prepared the ground for the seed which others would sow.

The organizational history of Universalism is inextricably bound up with the life of John Murray (1741-1815). Murray, the son of a stern, devout Calvinist family, was born in Alton, England, the year de Benneville arrived in Pennsylvania. When John was ten years old, the family moved to Ireland, and it was in Ireland that John encountered Methodism. It should be remembered that Methodism, at this point, was not so much a Protestant denomination as it was a school, a style, a method for pursuing the Christian life. Murray became a Methodist and soon was made youth leader and song leader among the Methodists. He was greatly successful in his new-found community, though he confessed in his autobiography that his irrepressible cheerfulness seemed inconsistent with strong religious convictions.[55]

After his father's death, Murray became an occasional preacher among the Methodists, a role he enjoyed. However, his self-doubts were never completely stilled. After moving to London, where he was affiliated with the congregation centered upon George Whitefield, he confessed that he found himself attracted by a "life of dissipation." In addition to his Methodist community, he took the opportunity provided by the great city to visit a variety of churches. In the course of this exploration, he encountered the ideas of a preacher named James Relly.

Relly (1722-1778) was Welsh and had converted to Methodism in 1741, the year of Murray's birth. He had served as an evangelist in Wales for a period of time, and then came to London in 1750. In London, Relly broke with his Methodist affiliations as a result of having adopted a universalist position which he explained in a book entitled UNION: OR A TREATISE ON THE CONSANGUINITY AND AFFINITY BETWEEN CHRIST AND HIS CHURCH.

Relly accepted most of the Christian system, including the doctrines of original sin, and vicarious atonement by Christ on the cross. The twist he gave those doctrines, however, centered upon what he believed was the mystical union of all people in Adam, and in Christ, the second Adam. Relly insisted that all of humanity, all succeeding generations of the human race, were contained within Adam when he sinned against God. All humanity participated in that sin, and therefore all of humanity stands in need of redemption. It was this sin which Christ died to redeem. Just as all human beings were present in Adam when he sinned, so all human beings were present in Christ when he paid the price of that sin. His death was sufficient payment for all sin, and therefore, human redemption has already been accomplished and human beings need only acknowledge and rejoice in that fact. It is not so much that all will be saved, but that in the mystical union of Christ with his church and with humanity, all have been saved.

This was the message Relly preached in London, the message with which he gathered a devoted congregation.[56] This was the message Murray encountered, and found less than convincing. Nevertheless, something in that message lodged deep within Murray. He withdrew from his activities as a lay preacher, although he remained involved in the religious activities of his Methodist congregation. It was also true that at the time, Murray's energies and interests were directed elsewhere. In 1769, he married Eliza Neale.

The Methodist congregation unwittingly upset Murray's delicate balance when they charged him to recover a member of the congregation who had become a Rellyan. Murray and several others of the congregation sought out the lost soul and attempted to convince her that Relly's Universalism could not be true. Rather than meekly submitting, the young woman met challenge with challenge, query with query, until Murray found himself bested at every point by her arguments. He confessed that her remarks were unanswerable. Unable to prevail, Murray, at that moment determined that henceforth he would avoid all Universalists.

Apparently, however, something in the unassailable nature of the Universalist message grabbed Murray and would not let him go. He went to hear Relly; he read his book; then he went to hear him again. In the end, Murray was convinced and became a Universalist. For a while, he was an active participant in both groups, attempting to hold his Universalist convictions as a private matter while continuing his ties to Methodism. Eventually, however, he was driven to proclaim his Universalism and was ejected from the Methodist congregation, though by a very narrow margin.

Murray now entered into a time of profound personal troubles. He was arrested and imprisoned for debt, and subsequently released. His infant child became ill and died. His wife, Eliza, fell ill. Struggling to support his wife and provide medical care, his debts begin to pile up again. Then Eliza died. Neither religion nor human community offered him solace. His eyesight began to fail and, alone in the world, John Murray found himself contemplating suicide as the only reasonable alternative open to him. At this juncture he encountered a traveler from America, and a new plan of action emerged. Rather than suicide, Murray would find another way to give up on religion and on the world. He resolved to "bury himself in the New World."

In July of 1770, Murray boarded the ship "Hand In Hand" and sailed for the port of New York. Three days out of New York, the vessel encountered another ship carrying word that the port of New York was closed to all English imports. Upon hearing this news, the Captain of the "Hand In Hand" decided to head, instead, to Philadelphia. There he discovered that the news concerning New York had been wrong, and so he set sail again for his original destination. Off the New Jersey coast, the ship ran aground at Barnegat Bay.

In an effort to lighten the ship and free it from the shoals, cargo was transferred to a sloop, and Murray was put in charge of this vessel. Murray now found himself becalmed off the Jersey coast. He went ashore in search of provisions for the crew, and there met a local resident named Thomas Potter.

The Potter family had originally been Quakers in Rhode Island, and had later become Rogerine Baptists. The Rogerine Baptists placed great emphasis on the conviction that Christ died for all. Potter himself was illiterate but deeply religious. He had had the Bible read to him, and had found therein reinforcement for his mystical Universalism. It is unlikely that the Ephrata Cloister's missionaries who traveled to Barnagat Bay in 1744 could have failed to encounter Potter who was living in the area at the time. Indeed on his estate Potter had built a meeting-house for itinerant preachers.

When Potter encountered Murray in September of 1770, he urged him to preach in his meeting-house. Murray, having lost all confidence in religion, and having come to American to bury himself in its vast wilderness, had no intention of ever preaching again. Potter, however, was insistent, and in the end, Murray agreed that if the ship remained becalmed, he would preach in Potter's meeting house on Sunday. On September 30, 1770, John Murray preached his first sermon in North America—a date which subsequent generations would fix as the beginning of Universalism in America.

His audience enthusiastically received Murray's sermon. Acquitting his responsibility for the sloop that had been entrusted to his care, Murray took advantage of the freshening breeze and sailed to New York. He then returned to New Jersey to preach again. Before long, the word of his preaching had spread and he found himself receiving requests to preach in a variety of places. He accepted invitations to preach in New York and in Philadelphia. As his fame grew, so did the opposition. In 1771, he had preached in a Baptist church in Philadelphia. On his next visit to that city, all the churches were closed to him.

In 1772, Murray preached in Connecticut and Rhode Island. The following year, he was back in Philadelphia and preached also in Maryland, Delaware, and in Boston, to large crowds. His message was deliberately oblique, lest he be rejected before given a hearing. However, it was clear enough that on occasion he was attacked with eggs and stones.

In 1774, Murray visited Winthrop Sargent in Gloucester, Massachusetts. Sargent was part of a small group in the Massachusetts seaport already acquainted with Rellyan thought, having read his book, UNION, which had been brought to their attention by a British sailor. So taken with the book were they that a group in the town had begun to meet separately from the Parish Church for the purpose of discussing the religious insights and issues raised by the book. Murray, pleased to find a group of people open to his message, accepted the invitation to make Gloucester his home.

In the political and social confusion of those years in Massachusetts, Murray was looked upon with suspicion. He was charged with being a papist, intent upon undermining the established church and delivering the community to Rome. He was charged with being an agent of Lord North and the British government, seeking to fasten the yoke of the Anglican Church firmly about the neck of the rebellious colonists. Unable to make either charge stick, the town eventually charged him with vagrancy. In response to that charge, Winthrop Sargent deeded Murray sufficient property to make him a freeholder of the town and, thus free him from the threat of prosecution.

In 1775, Murray left Gloucester briefly when he was appointed chaplain of the Rhode Island Brigade of the Continental Army. Even in the midst of war, he was not free from the attacks of opponents. Orthodox ministers sought his removal from the chaplaincy, appealing to General George Washington. Washington responded by confirming Murray in his office. However, after brief service, illness forced Murray's retirement from the post.

Back in Gloucester, he set about to work for the relief of those who had been impoverished by the war. Even in this philanthropic endeavor he drew suspicion. Charged before the Committee of Public Safety as subversive of the public welfare, eventually he was acquitted of those charges.

In the meantime, the small group of Universalists in Gloucester continued to meet for the study and discussion of religious topics. Eventually sixteen members of First Parish Church were suspended from the church for failure to attend services. They chose to worship privately, and to ask Murray to preach for them. So successful were these services that the group determined to build a meeting-house on property donated by Winthrop Sargent. The building was dedicated on December 25, 1780, with John Murray preaching. This congregation, the Independent Church of Christ in Gloucester, Massachusetts, was the first Universalist church in North America. Among the thirty-one men and thirty women who comprised its list of charter members was one Gloucester Dalton, an African American who had been a slave.

Having been suspended from First Parish, and having created their own church with its own building, the members of the Independent Church discovered that under Massachusetts law they were yet required to continue paying taxes for the support of First Parish Church. Feeling this law unjust, some members of the new congregation refused to pay the taxes. In retaliation, the town seized and sold the property of members of the Universalist congregation, claiming that the Universalists were not a church, were not incorporated, did not pay a minister, and were, in truth, nothing more than a collection of dissenters.

In response, the congregation prevailed upon Murray to accept a salary, a proposal which Murray had been loathe to embrace, believing that as a minister he should rely on the freely given support of those who heard his message. Then, in 1783, the Universalists brought suit, seeking to be freed from the burden of supporting a congregation to which they no longer belonged. The case dragged through the courts for three years before the Universalists won the right to have their taxes used to support their own church. This was the first step in a long process by which Universalists would seek the total separation of church and state in Massachusetts.

Frustrated at every turn, Murray's opponents now attacked from another direction. Murray was accused of having been improperly ordained and therefore of performing weddings illegally. The courts hearing the charge found Murray guilty and fined him 50 pounds. Murray decided that this would be a convenient time to return to England for a visit until the Massachusetts legislature acted to reverse the court decision. (On the return voyage he met John and Abigail Adams, who were passengers on the same ship.) On Christmas day, Murray was re-ordained, thus laying to rest the charge of irregularity which had been placed against him.

Having returned to Gloucester, Murray married Judith Sargent Stevens, the widowed daughter of Winthrop Sargent. Judith Sargent Stevens Murray was a formidable woman in her own right. She was one of the earliest of the feminists, a popular and successful writer who often used a pseudonym. Indeed, a cousin once claimed that "Judith wrote poetry by the acre." Above all, she was an ardent and vigilant supporter and defender of John Murray.[57]

In 1793, Murray accepted an invitation to become the minister of a group of Universalists in Boston. He and Judith moved to Boston and served the congregation there until his death. Disabled by a stroke in 1809, he died in 1815, leaving behind an incomplete autobiography, which his wife, Judith, carefully and lovingly finished and saw through the press.

John Murray was the great apostle of Universalism, but he was not the only spokesman for the larger gospel. Just as he had been preceded by the German Brethren and by de Benneville, so he labored in the context of a time ready for the message he delivered. And the times raised up others to join him in his ministry.[58] By 1785 there were enough Universalist congregations to justify the calling of a conference in Oxford, Massachusetts, for the purpose of providing the new movement with a mechanism for mutual support and consultation. Nine laymen and ministers, representing six churches in Massachusetts and one in Rhode Island were present at this gathering.

Among those in attendance at the Oxford meeting was Elhanan Winchester (1751-1797). Winchester was born in Brookline, Massachusetts, the son of a farmer and shoemaker who was also a deacon in the parish church. Though he had little formal education, Elhanan had an innate talent for languages. Through self-study, he mastered Latin, Biblical Greek and Hebrew, and a smattering of French.[59] At nineteen, as a result of a revival experience, Elhanan began to preach to congregations gathered in his father's home. In 1770, he became a Baptist and was ordained a Baptist minister. Five years later, he settled on the Great Pee Dee River in South Carolina, where he served as minister to a Baptist congregation. In 1780, on his way from South Carolina to Massachusetts, he happened through Philadelphia. The Baptist church there was without a minister at the time. Winchester preached in the church and was so well received that he decided to stay.

While in South Carolina, Winchester had read THE EVERLAST-ING GOSPEL, and a conviction of the truth of universalism began to develop within him. In Philadelphia he read THE RESTITUTION OF ALL THINGS by Sir George Stonehouse and his universalist sympathies grew. At first he was reluctant to claim the label, but ultimately it became clear to the congregation that Winchester had embraced the teaching of universal salvation. Although he was strongly supported in the ensuing controversy by George de Benneville, in the end, Winchester and his supporters were excommunicated from the church in 1785.

Winchester responded by establishing the Society of Universal Baptists, a church he served until 1787. In that year he traveled to England, where he preached to various congregations, and, for a brief time, served as James Relly's successor in London. While in England, he published an attack on slavery in North America, an address he had written while in South Carolina and which he had delivered publicly in Virginia. He also published DIALOGUES ON UNIVERSAL SALVATION, which was widely read in America.

Winchester returned to America in 1794, impoverished and in ill health. He preached in New England, and for a brief time was back in Philadelphia. He presided over the Oxford, Massachusetts, meeting of the New England Convention of Universalists in 1795. Two years later, at the age of forty-six, Elhanan Winchester died.

During these years, Universalism continued to spread, and the need for an organizational structure became increasingly urgent. In 1790, at a convention held in Philadelphia, Universalists adopted articles of faith, a statement of principles and made recommendations for church governance. A major force behind this meeting was Dr. Benjamin Rush, a signer of the Declaration of Independence, friend of Adams, Jefferson and Priestley, physician to George Washington, and the man known to history as the "father of American psychiatry."

Rush had been a member of Elhanan Winchester's congregation. He was the author of the first official statement of Universalist beliefs. In the process, he left an indelible mark on subsequent Universalist history. Rush insisted that Universalism and republican government were part of the same unfolding process, and that social action is an inescapable consequence of Universalist faith. In 1790, he laid out the program to which Universalists would return again and again—opposition to slavery, a commitment to temperance, a concern for prison reform, a passion for peace, and involvement in work with the poor which would foreshadow the social gospel movement two centuries later.[60]

In 1793, once more in Oxford, the New England Universalist Convention was organized. This body, with several name changes would continue in existence until, in 1961, as the Universalist Church of America, it would merge with the American Unitarian Association to form the Unitarian Universalist Association.

It was at a meeting of the New England Convention, presided over by Elhanan Winchester, that a young man, Hosea Ballou, was suddenly and spontaneously ordained, when Winchester pressed a Bible to his chest and commanded him to preach the gospel.

Ballou was born in 1771, the son of a farmer and unpaid Baptist preacher in Richmond, New Hampshire. He was raised in a strict Calvinist household, but as a teen-ager, he happened to hear Caleb Rich preach. Rich was a radical Universalist, believing that all punishment for sin was confined to this life. He had embraced this position as early as 1773, and preached his faith throughout New England. Rich's independence and his radical Universalism resulted in strained relations with John Murray and the more conservative Universalists, who held that while punishment was not eternal, nonetheless there would be a finite term of punishment for sin after death.

Rich succeeded in planting seeds of doubt concerning orthodox religion in Hosea Ballou's mind. Although he joined his father's church in 1790, he could never fully embrace the orthodox doctrines his father preached. That same year, he confessed his Universalism to his father, and was excommunicated from the church. Nor was this the only defection the elder Ballou would endure. Hosea's older brother, David, not only embraced Universalism, but began to preach "the larger gospel."

In 1791, Hosea's formal education came to an end. Added all together, he had had not more than three years of sporadic formal education. Unhampered by this fact, Hosea followed in David's footsteps and began to preach universal salvation. In these early years, he read Ethan Allen's book, REASON, THE ONLY ORACLE OF MAN, and was profoundly influenced by the deist, rationalist thought it represented.

After his spontaneous ordination at the hands of Elhanan Winchester,[61] Ballou continued to preach in various places. In 1798 he was engaged to supply the pulpit for John Murray. Judith Murray, sitting in the congregation, was surprised to hear a doctrine so different from that preached by her husband. The story is told that Mrs. Murray passed a note to the choir director and asked him to inform the congregation that the doctrine heard from the pulpit on that day was not the doctrine usually presented from that pulpit. Ballou politely urged the congregation to attend to Mrs. Murray's disclaimer and brought the service to an end.

The incident serves to illustrate the theological evolution occurring within Universalism, as it was emerging and growing and organizing in New England and New York. John Murray had never deviated from the teachings of James Relly. He remained a trinitarian and he accepted original sin, atonement through the death of Christ, and the inerrancy of the scripture as central to his theological system. He taught that there would be punishment after death for the sin of disbelief, and that only when sufficient punishment had been endured would all be restored to harmony with God.

When the Universalists adopted a profession of faith in 1803—the Winchester Profession—its tenets were shaped to be acceptable to Murray.[62] But even then differences within the movement were strong enough that the Universalists attached a freedom clause allowing room for those differences.[63] Over the years, the Winchester Profession with its freedom clause was valued as much for its ambiguity as for the doctrines it proclaimed.

Caleb Rich had parted company with Murray over the question of future punishment, Rich insisting that punishment for sin occurs in this life not in some future state. His young protege, Hosea Ballou would move even further from the teachings of the venerable patriarch. Influenced by his reading of Ethan Allen, Ballou sought to structure a theology that was rational and yet consistent with scripture. That effort resulted in A TREATISE ON ATONEMENT, published in 1805. In that work, Ballou, using homely examples and sharp wit, argued that religion is to be approached through the scriptures as interpreted by reason. He insisted that God could not be inconsistent, and therefore he would not endow humanity with reason and then present a revelation that was incompatible with that reason. Fundamental to his argument was the insistence that God is not a wrathful deity, but rather a loving deity; therefore, Christ came not to atone for some ancient, infinite human sin, but rather to reveal divine love to the human community. Christ suffered for men, not instead of them, for God does not need to be reconciled to humanity; rather human beings need to be reconciled to God.

Ballou grounded his Universalism in the insistence that as God is unlimited, so God's love is also without bounds. It embraces all, and because God is all-powerful, it is not possible for any human being to frustrate God's love or God's design. In some ways, Ballou presented a system which offered a Calvinism turned on its head. However, his commitment to reason led him to deny the doctrine of the trinity. He argued that if the Godhead consists of three distinct persons, each infinite, then the Godhead amounts to infinity times three—an impossible and unreasonable concept. "If on the other hand, the three persons be not infinite, the addition of a thousand more like them would not add up to infinity." His conviction that a rational God would not present an irrational revelation led him to reject the doctrine of the trinity.

THE TREATISE ON ATONEMENT's systematic attack on the doctrine of the trinity came a decade and a half before the Unitarians embraced that name as an appropriate reflection of their theological position. The "Treatise" provoked an immediate and sweeping theological reconstruction among Universalists. Ballou's book by-passed Murray theologically, and established its author as a central figure in the emerging movement. Within ten years of the publication of the TREATISE, the Universalists had become unitarian in their theology, and committed to Ballou's rationalism. Indeed, by 1815 only two Universalist ministers continued to resist the new theology.

It would be reasonable to assume that the liberal Christians who were part of the emergent Unitarian movement might welcome the appearance of a potential ally in New England. However, the Universalists came from the wrong side of the tracks, in a number of ways. Murray, Winchester, Rich, Ballou and others who proclaimed the Universalist gospel were all seen as itinerants rather than as part of the settled religious order. Their ordinations were irregular, to say the least. They had little or no education—Ballou not more than three years of formal schooling. Their congregations were drawn from disaffected Baptists, Methodists, Quakers, and German sects— all of them churches serving the lower social classes. And, of course, they attacked the doctrine of hell which many Liberal Christians saw as a useful support for social order, whether or not it was theologically defensible. The Liberal Christians who would become Unitarians interpreted early Universalism as part of the revivalist phenomenon, another form of the enthusiastic religion which had aroused so much tumult and had so unsettled the standing order of things in New England. They failed to see that the two groups had much, if anything in common. As a consequence, Unitarians failed to welcome Universalism, despite the fact that the Universalists were staunch unitarians.

In 1817, after Murray's Death, Ballou moved to Boston to become minister of the Second Universalist Society. He was to become one of the most popular preachers in that city, as well as a central figure in his own denomination. He edited THE UNIVERSALIST MAGAZINE and later a scholarly journal, THE UNIVERSALIST EXPOSITOR. In 1821 he co-edited a hymn book for the denomination.[64] So beloved a figure was he that later generations of Universalists would refer to him as "Father" Ballou, an honorific that he shared with John Murray and several other early Universalist worthies.

CONTROVERSY AND SCHISM

Ballou, despite his lack of formal education, and despite the fact that Harvard Students who came to hear him often could not get past his rural accent to his thoughts, had an abiding concern for theological issues. In 1811, he and several of his Universalist colleagues organized a conference for mutual edification and religious discussion. As originally conceived, the group would meet annually to hear papers and discuss issues, and then would publish the proceedings. The conference ceased after only one volume of proceedings. Eight years later, Ballou and the Rev. Edward Turner determined to revive the project.

Casting about for a discussion topic that might excite some interest, Turner and Ballou determined to discuss future punishment—the very topic that had caused the estrangement between Murray and Caleb Rich. It was decided that one of them would defend the proposition that there is a limited period of punishment for sin after death, while the other would argue that all punishment is confined to this life. Ballou allowed Turner to choose which position to defend, and found himself left with the defense of the position that there is to be no punishment after death.

What began as an attempt to stimulate thought and discussion among the ministers of the denomination ended by generating a storm of controversy in the movement—the Restorationist Controversy. A bitter debate developed over whether "death and glory" Universalism—the position Ballou came to be identified with—or "restoration" Universalism—the teaching that only after a period of punishment would souls be restored to harmony with God—best defined the Universalist movement.

By 1822, the debate, which had drawn much of its strength from a concern that teaching a lack of future retribution might weaken the moral order, took a new turn and became bitter and destructive, as personal animosity emerged and added new fuel to the raging fire of theological difference. Ballou, alarmed at the consequences of his undertaking, attempted to close off the debate but without success. In 1830 a schism occurred within Universalism, with the founding of the Massachusetts Association of Universalist Restorationists, and the separation of some twelve societies from the New England Convention of Universalists.

The Restorationists meet separately for the ten years between 1831 and 1841 and then faded from history, many of them becoming Unitarians, who, by this time were Restorationists themselves.

Most of the Universalists remained with the New England Convention, and it would appear that the "Ultra-Universalists", the so-called
"death and glory" Universalists carried the day. But in truth many
of the Universalists who remained with the main body were quietly
sympathetic to the Restorationist position; they simply did not feel
it important enough to separate over the issue. Later in the century,
Restorationism would become the dominant position.

Universalism did not evolve in a social or an intellectual vacuum.
Universalists were affected by many of the same intellectual currents that swept the rest of the country in the mid-nineteenth century. Thus, for example, the challenge of Transcendentalism represented in the thinking of Emerson and Parker was not confined to
Unitarianism. As we have suggested, Emerson had transferred spiritual and moral authority from its traditional base in scripture and
tradition to nature, the Over-soul, and the individual experience of
the world. Parker had stripped Christianity of its claim to special
revelation and had insisted that truth cannot be confined within its
traditional Christian formulations. Universalism could not insulate
itself from the challenge these ideas presented.

Indeed, Universalism had its own radical prefiguration of many
of these ideas in the person of one of its ministers, Abner Kneeland.
Ordained to the Universalist ministry in 1804, over the years
Kneeland developed doubts about the central tenets of Christianity,
even as interpreted by the Universalists. After 25 years in the ministry, he left Universalism and became a popular lecturer for the Free
Thought movement in Boston where, it is said, he would read passages from Leviticus concerning menstruation, then hurl the Bible
across the room, proclaiming that it was unfit reading. Kneeland
combined his theological radicalism with a radical social vision. He
was a thoroughgoing champion of equal rights. He also advocated
inter-racial marriage and the abolition of slavery. Needless to say,
the Universalists, as a group, were embarrassed by his teachings.
Though Kneeland left the Universalist ministry in 1829, in the

public's eye, he remained a Universalist minister; so at one point the editor of the Universalist Trumpet asked him to declare himself in a way which would make it clear that he was no longer a representative of the denomination. Kneeland replied:

"Dear Sir: You observed to me the other day, that people still considered me a Universalist, and said to me 'If you will acknowledge that you are not, I will publish it.' ...I shall now answer you....

I still hold to universal philanthropy, universal benevolence, and universal charity. In those respects I am still a Universalist. Neither do I believe in punishment after death; so in this also I agree with Universalists. But as it respects all other of their religious notions in relation to another world, or a supposed state of conscious existence, I do not believe in any of them; so that in this respect I am no more a universalist than I am an orthodox Christian. As for instance.

1. Universalists believe in a god which I do not; but believe that their god, with all his moral attributes, (aside from nature itself,) is nothing more than a chimera of their own imagination.

2. Universalists believe in Christ, which I do not; but believe that the whole story concerning him is as much a fable and a fiction, as that of the god Prometheus, the tragedy of whose death is said to have been acted on the stage in the theatre at Athens, 500 years before the christian era.

3. Universalists believe in miracles, which I do not; but believe that every pretension to them can either be accounted for on natural principles or else is to be attributed to mere trick and imposture.

4. Universalists believe in the resurrection of the dead, in immortality and eternal life, which I do not; but believe that all life is mortal, that death is an eternal extinction of life to the individual who possesses it, and that no individual

life is, ever was, or ever will be eternal.

Hence as Universalists no longer wish to consider me as being of their faith, and I no longer wish to be considered as belonging to their order, as it relates to a belief in things unseen, I hope the above four articles will be sufficient to distinguish me from them and them from me. I profess to believe in all realities of which I can form any rational conception, while they believe in what I believe to be mere ideal nothings to which they give both 'a location and a name.'...[65]

Not only was his statement sufficient to distinguish him from the Universalists, it proved effective enough to have him jailed for blasphemy in 1838—the last person in Massachusetts to be punished for that crime. Neither Parker nor Emerson had ever gone so far. Channing, though offended by Kneeland's opinions, petitioned for his release from jail. Upon his release, Kneeland removed to Iowa, where he became one of the founders of that state.

Abner Kneeland, it must be admitted was the exception rather than the rule among Universalists. Although Mary Livermore was a strong supporter of Theodore Parker, most Universalists rejected Parker, Emerson, and the Transcendentalism they taught. Indeed, in 1847, conservatives within the Universalist movement sought to defend against infidelity by requiring faith in the Biblical revelation, including the miracles, the death and the resurrection of Jesus. Liberals sought to block any such effort by offering the Winchester Profession with its freedom clause as sufficient. In the end, the conservatives prevailed. In 1848 the General Convention adopted a resolution affirming that the Bible contains a special revelation from God which is sufficient for faith and practice. It would seem clear that the need to adopt such a statement is evidence that some of the clergy were beginning to have doubts about the inerrancy of scripture.

Resolutions of the General Convention were to prove a weak defense against the emergence of new convictions. In 1859 Charles Darwin published his theory of evolution. Conservative Universalists immediately saw this new form of infidelity as a threat. However, it was a Universalist scholar, Orello Cone, who introduced both Higher Criticism of the Bible and Darwinian thought to the American Academic world. Before long Thomas B. Thayer, the preeminent Universalist theologian of his day, would be insisting that Darwin, rather than representing infidelity, proves the existence of God as mind, as on-going process.

While these developments were occurring within the theological and intellectual life of the movement, Universalism was showing a remarkable pattern of growth. Unlike their Unitarian cousins, the Universalists were evangelical in their nature. They carried their gospel far and wide and gathered societies and churches in small towns and large cities. Nor were they reluctant to debate their orthodox adversaries with skill and vigor.

Beginning de novo in the late eighteenth century, by 1835 Universalism was proclaimed as "the reigning heresy of the day" by the Boston Recorder. The statistics however are problematical. A conservative estimate suggests that in 1800 there were 22 ministers. Within twenty years, Universalists had spread from urban centers to the interior and to rural areas, and counted 200 societies or churches, mostly in New England and New York (50 more than the Unitarians). In 1832, the American Almanac listed Universalism as the sixth largest denomination in the country, with about 500,000 adherents. In 1840, they were credited with three percent of the total population of the country, which would have represented about 700,000 Universalists. However, the records of the denomination itself never counted more than 55,000 members, and that number may have been inflated.[66] One thing seems clear beyond all dispute: by 1850 growth beyond population growth had stopped.

THE SOCIAL AGENDA

The end of the period of rapid growth may be explained in a variety of ways: Perhaps internal debates functioned to sap the strength of a movement which had offered a single, provocative proclamation—that there is no Hell. Or perhaps the very success of the Universalist movement caused it to lust after respectability, thus weakening the distinction between it and other religious communities. Or perhaps the Universalists succeeded in convincing the wider religious community to drop the emphasis on eternal punishment, thus allowing main-stream Protestantism to take over the theological ground the Universalists had staked out as their own. More likely, the decline in Universalist fortunes may be related to the growing social crisis that would result in the Civil War. As that terrible ordeal approached, Universalist attention and energy were diverted from their primary religious agenda and focused strongly on the social and political and moral challenges confronting the nation.

Universalists brought a peculiar vision to the social agenda. Harking back to the convictions of Benjamin Rush, the Universalists saw an inescapable social imperative in the theology that defined them. Rush had pioneered in organizing Sunday Schools to provide basic education for the children of the poor in Philadelphia. Centered among rural, poor and relatively uneducated people, Universalists soon saw a need for the establishment of educational institutions. Though proud of their "native wit and reason," they were stung by the charge that they were socially and intellectually inferior. What is more, most educational institutions were avowedly sectarian, teaching religious doctrines as well as more secular skills. Universalist children, exposed to such schools were constantly subjected to efforts at converting them to orthodox faiths.

In response, Universalists early sought to establish non-sectarian schools and academies. These institutions were open to all and sought to provide young people with an education that did not include sectarian indoctrination. Most of these schools were also designed to provide education for girls and women. Inevitably the concern for education would extend to higher education. Among the schools founded by Universalists were Tufts Unitersity, St.

Lawrence University, Buchtel College (now Akron University), Lombard College, and Throop Institute (now Cal Tech). Theological education, though regarded with suspicion by Father Ballou, would be offered by Crane Theological School at Tufts in Medford, Massachusetts; St. Lawrence Theological School in Canton, New York; and Ryder Divinity School in Chicago. Less formally, the Universalists sought to educate the public at large by establishing a publishing house and by founding some seventeen periodicals by 1860.

As we have already indicated, Universalists had a strong interest in the issue of separation of Church and State. The early history of the Gloucester Church had involved that congregation in a determined struggle for the right to support its own religious institution rather than be taxed to support the established church. The Universalists would continue this struggle, in coalition with other groups, until 1833 when the churches in Massachusetts would be disestablished and the separation of church and state finally accomplished[67]

Universalists, from the early part of the nineteenth century saw prison reform and the end of capital punishment as imperatives growing directly out of their religious convictions. Universalists argued that just as nothing any human being might do could suffice to separate that person from God's love, so no act could free human beings from their obligation to offer unconditional love. Prisons should be places of reform and all punishment should be directed toward reform rather than vengeance. Prisoners who had completed their sentences needed assistance rather than rejection. Debt should no longer be punished with imprisonment. Charles Spear (1801-1863) gave up his parish work to focus on a ministry of social concerns, devoting himself especially to prison reform. He was joined in his work by George W. Quimby (1811-1844) who crusaded for reform in his newspapers and in a number of books.

Universalists saw capital punishment as a failure of faith in God's ability to renew, regenerate, reform even the most reprobate character. Beginning with Rush and Winchester, the Universalists argued that as God did not give up on anyone, so it behooved human beings to refuse to give up hope for human regeneration. It is said that the Universalists unquestionably provided more "gallows reformers" than any other denomination. For fifty years, from 1802-1852, Universalists maintained a steady and ultimately successful campaign to change the laws regarding capital punishment in Massachusetts, and in 1836, the General Convention of Universalists broke their strong reluctance to interfere with the legislature of any state to urge the abolition of the death penalty in the United States.

In the years between 1846 and 1866, the Universalists had sought to address the social concerns that had emerged among them by a vehicle called the General Reform Association. This separate organization represented an attempt to respond to social issues without violating the sense that secular concerns may not be the appropriate concern of churches.

The Association adopted a forty item agenda. In the area of economic and domestic relations, they expressed concern for slavery and the "colored race," the domestic slave trade, wages, marriage, women's rights, etc. In international relations they were concerned about war, commerce, colonization, Indians, foreign slave trade, rights of seamen, etc. In the arena of social institutions and habits, they focused on temperance, education, politics and laws, the press, amusements, the poor, etc. And in an area entitled Offenders, Irresponsible and Unfortunate Persons, they focused on capital punishment, prison discipline, juvenile offenders, debtors' prisons, dueling, the insane, etc.

Important as these issues were, however, the attention of Universalists, and most of the rest of the nation, was directed to the issue of slavery as the crisis of the Union approached. Again, opposition to slavery had emerged early within Universalism. Rush had opposed slavery in 1773; Winchester had made his opposition known in 1774 and again in 1788. The Philadelphia Convention, under the guidance of Benjamin Rush, had opposed slavery in 1790.

The Universalists, however, sought to be moderate in their approach to the issue. True to their theology, they were reluctant to demonize anyone, including the slave owners and the slave traders. Seeing everyone entangled in this tragic circumstance—both slaves and slave-holders alike—as victims, Universalists struggled to find a peaceful end to the peculiar institution, and urged that strident denunciations would result only in a strengthening of resistance.

In Maine in 1841, finding themselves unwelcome in the mainstream abolitionist movement that was dominated by Congregationalists and Presbyterians, the Universalist Association created its own abolitionist movement. Two years later, the General Convention of Universalists, meeting in Akron, Ohio, declared that slavery was inconsistent with Universalism, with justice and with Christian love and that it was pernicious to the enslaver and the enslaved alike.

The declaration by the Akron Convention was given wide coverage in the New York Tribune, whose editor, Horace Greeley, was, himself, a Universalist. The Herkimer Journal declared that this declaration made the Universalists the first "major denomination" to take a stand on the slavery issue. Within the denomination itself, the response was mixed: some felt that even on this important matter, a religious body ought not dabble in political issues. Others felt the convention had not gone far enough in its denunciation. Clearly, however, the Akron meeting had set Universalism on the path that it would walk for the next twenty years.

When the Fugitive Slave Laws—requiring the return of escaped slaves to their owners—were passed, various individuals and Universalist State Conventions called for civil disobedience as a response to laws judged to be immoral and unacceptable. In 1853, Universalists, with remarkable clarity of insight, noted that slavery was only the beginning of the problem, that Blacks would require help erasing the consequences of slavery and for that to happen, "we must conquer our miserable prejudices."

By the time the Civil War began in 1861, Universalists were strongly committed to the Union cause. Fifty Universalist ministers served as chaplains in the Union Army. In some cases, entire Sunday-school classes enrolled as volunteers in the Union cause, often following the lead of their teachers. It seemed symbolic that the first Union casualty of the war, Sumner Henry Needham, who was killed in the Baltimore Riots as the troops passed through that city in 1861, was a Universalist.

Nor was the army the only mechanism by which Universalists expressed their commitment to the Union cause and their opposition to slavery. In Richmond, Virginia, Rev. A. Bosserman, the Universalist minister, was the only clergyman in the city to support the Union cause. He was arrested, imprisoned, threatened with death, and eventually sent north in exile. Mary A. Livermore, working with Henry Whitney Bellows, made the U.S. Sanitary Commission an effective force in responding to the needs of the soldiers. And, of course, the most famous of the Universalists, Clara Barton, "the angel of the battlefield," defied danger and death itself in order to minister to the needs of the wounded and dying soldiers.

The war would change the nation in ways no one could foresee. Women's rights, which had been a long-standing concern among Universalists, dating at least from the influence of Judith Sargent Murray, and of Benjamin Rush, who had advocated education for women in 1787, would receive greater attention as a consequence of the upheavals of the civil war.

It is important to note that with the exception of Tufts, all Universalist schools had been open to women from their founding. What is more, women had played an important part in Universalist development from Murray's first encounter with the fallen-away Methodist who bested him at every turn as he sought to show her the errors of her ways.

The early history of women in the Universalist ministry can be traced to 1810, at which time Maria Cook was preaching among the Universalists in western Pennsylvania and New York. A year later, she was issued a letter of Fellowship by the New York Universalists. In 1838 a Universalist, Mary Ann Church, was described as the only woman preacher in upper Canada (now Ontario). In the same period, Sally Dunn was preaching among the Universalists in Maine. In 1857, Lydia Jenkins was preaching among Universalists in New York State, and they granted her a letter of Fellowship the following year. Recent evidence suggests that she was ordained in 1860.

The history of women in the Universalist Ministry continued in 1863 with the ordination of two women, Olympia Brown and Augusta J. Chapin. Brown, a graduate of Antioch College and of St. Lawrence Theological School, had completed her degree despite the efforts of the officials of the school and the denomination to discourage her. In the summer of 1863, she was ordained by the St. Lawrence Association of Universalists in Malone, NY, and has been celebrated as the first woman in the United States whose ordination was officially sanctioned and recognized by a denominational body. After her ordination, Brown went on to serve congregations in Massachusetts, Connecticut (where P.T. Barnum was one of her parishioners) and Wisconsin. Eventually, she would leave the full-time ministry to devote her efforts to the cause of women's suffrage. Olympia Brown would be the only one of the major women's suffrage leaders to live to see women granted the vote.

The same year that Olympia Brown was ordained, Augusta J. Chapin was ordained. Although she had had less formal education than Olympia Brown, Chapin had been preaching in the mid-west for several years prior to her formal ordination. She devoted her entire life to the Universalist ministry, serving churches throughout the midwest, and the far west, as well as New York state. Chapin chaired the Women's Committee on Religious Congresses of the World Parliament of Religions, held in Chicago in conjunction with the world's fair in 1893. A few months earlier, she had been honored with the Doctor of Divinity degree by Lombard College—the first woman to receive that degree.

Following in the footsteps of these pioneers, many women entered the Universalist ministry in the last third of the nineteenth century. Phoebe Hanaford was the first woman to serve as chaplain of a legislative body (Connecticut). Caroline Augusta Soule was the Universalist's first woman missionary, serving Universalist congregations in Scotland from 1875-1903.

This thrust of women into the ministry was part of a larger social development. As often is the case with wars, the Civil War disrupted society in ways no one anticipated. The effectiveness and competence of women like Mary Livermore and Clara Barton was not lost on their less famous sisters. Women would not only demand the right to vote, but they would demand greater control over many aspects of their lives.

When the Universalists decided to hold a massive celebration of the centennial of the arrival of John Murray on this continent, the Women's Centenary Society was established primarily as a vehicle for funding the event. The women organized effectively and demonstrated their ability to raise substantial amounts of money. After the celebration of the Centennial in 1870, they decided that the temporary organization should become permanent. The men generously offered to take over the responsibility for managing the financial affairs of the new organization. The women graciously declined the offer. They could raise money and they could manage it and they could decide how it would be used! The Women's Centenary Society became the Association of Universalist Women—said to be the first continent-wide women's organization in America. As the century drew to a close, the Women's Association became a major force in missionary efforts and other special outreach programs within the denomination. After merger between the Unitarians and the Universalists, it would become part of the Unitarian Universalist

Women's Federation (UUWF).

Despite this illustrious history of strong, committed, competent and determined women, it must be admitted that action for women's rights often remained a matter of individual effort rather than of denominational votes and resolutions. More than once, efforts to put the Universalists on record in support of equal rights for women were tabled.

ORGANIZING THE MOVEMENT

The Civil War had served in other ways to create a new consciousness among the American people. It has been noted that before that vast upheaval, it was common to refer to "The United States, they," after the war the common usage was "The United States, it." The war offered an unforgettable sense of broadened loyalties. Old boundaries of thought were broken. Old habits and relationships were shattered. The period after the war became a time to create and establish new structures more reflective of the broadened national sense. The Universalists responded by attempting to reshape their denominational organization.

The women had raised $35,000 in one year to finance the great Centennial celebration in 1870. Twelve thousand people, including 242 ministers gathered in Gloucester, Massachusetts to observe the one hundredth anniversary of Murray's arrival in New Jersey. There was preaching and speeches, including formal greetings from the Unitarians. In addition, the General Convention of Universalists held a formal meeting.

The 116 delegates from the various state conventions were presented with plans for reforming the denominational structure. Eventually, the meeting adopted a new constitution, which specified a three level hierarchy. At the local level was the parish, which belonged to a state convention. That convention was made up of the ministers of churches, lay delegates from churches, and the officers of the convention. The state convention had the power to issue letters of fellowship to ministers, to ordain ministers, and to discipline ministers. They were charged also with raising funds for the denomination, keeping careful statistics, maintaining and supporting Sunday schools and caring for indigent ministers.

The presidents, and secretaries of each of the state conventions and one ministerial and two lay people from each state convention served as delegates to the General Convention. The General Convention was authorized to hold trust funds, raise money, require reports, and to adjudicate disputes between state conventions and to serve as a court of final appeal for all cases of discipline. In this structure, the General Convention was seen as an ecclesiastic body, while the actual administrative functions were lodged with the state conventions.

The most controversial action by the Gloucester Convention came when, in approving the constitution, it reaffirmed the Winchester Profession of Faith, but dropped the historic liberty clause. Many people saw this as the signal of a move toward tighter organization, and toward theological conservatism and respectability.

That judgment seemed to have been ratified in the outcome of the trial for heresy of Rev. Herman Bisbee, minister of St. Anthony Church in Minnesota. Bisbee had been sympathetic to the views of Emerson and Parker and had begun to express that sympathy in his sermons. Tried on the charge that his teachings were not consistent with the Winchester Profession, Bisbee's fellowship had been revoked by the Minnesota State Convention.

This event, along with the dropping of the liberty clause demonstrated the determination of the Universalist leadership to safeguard its biblical, Christian basis. What it accomplished, in fact, was to usher in a twenty-year struggle to find a creed all could accept. So long as the liberty clause had been in place, no one had felt compelled to examine the Winchester Profession with great care. Once the clause was removed, every assertion of the Profession now assumed deep significance. In 1875, Rev. Abel C. Thomas objected to the phrase "finally restore" in the affirmation that God "will finally restore the whole family of mankind to holiness and happiness." The Rev. Mr. Thomas demanded to know what "finally restore" meant. Others were equally unclear about the meaning of the phrase "holiness and happiness."[68]

For two decades the denomination was confronted with growing unease with the Winchester Profession as a creedal document. Every attempt to change the language, to rephrase the assertions, to delete offending or controversial passages met with failure. In the end, the controversy was resolved by citing the Winchester profession, and including the liberty clause in a revised statement of conditions of fellowship in the Universalist General Convention.[69] With the action by the Convention in Boston in 1899 giving overwhelming approval to this restatement of traditional Universalist faith and of the freedom clause, the effort to craft a creed came to an end. Nonetheless, echoes of the struggle would be heard throughout the next fifty years as Universalists attempted to find an explanation for their numerical decline and a mechanism to reverse that decline.

While the convention struggled to define the faith in a clear and widely acceptable manner, the life of the movement did not stand still. In 1889, on the day before the opening of the General Convention in Lynn, Massachusetts, delegates from youth groups in fifty-six Universalist Churches met to create a national youth organization. In an effort to assist the young people in the Universalist churches to live "a serious Christian life," the Young People's Christian Union was established. With this action, the Universalists were breaking ground once more. The YPCU was "the first self initiated denominational youth organization. It preceded and set an example for the Baptists, Lutherans, Methodists and the Unitarians, who all followed suit within the next decade."[70]

In addition to its primary role of providing leadership and programs for the young, the Young People's Christian Union of the Universalist Church, along with the national women's organization soon became involved in raising funds to spread the faith, not only in the United States, but abroad as well. In 1890, the Universalist General Convention established a mission in Japan, and dispatched three missionaries who were charged with establishing schools and churches. The Japanese mission built four church buildings, established a school for Japanese girls, and developed friendly relations with the Unitarian missionaries who had arrived in Japan a year before the Universalists. Work with the Japanese continued until the outbreak of the Second World War, at which time the operation was transferred to native leadership. Following the war, the relationship was resumed through financial support and the building of a Universalist center. Eventually the Universalist Church in Japan became part of the Japan Free Religious Association.

It cannot be argued that the Universalist mission had a massive impact upon the Japanese nation. However, the mission may have had a subtle impact upon the development of American Universalism. For most of its history, Universalism had understood itself as a challenge to the narrow and partialist theology of mainstream Christianity. The mission of Universalism had been to provide a corrective to orthodox teachings about hell. In Japan, Universalist missionaries found themselves dealing with people who had little or no experience with Christian teachings, who had no investment in orthodox opinions about hell. Within American Universalism, this experience led to debates over whether it was necessary to be a partialist before one could understand the radical teaching of Universalism, or whether it was possible to skip that part of Christian history and experience. In short, the Japan mission may have contributed to a growing need to redefine Universalism in relation to Christian thought and to world religions.

Japan was not the only, or even the primary focus of Universalist missionary effort as the century came to a close. In 1891, Quillen Hamilton Shinn began his work as domestic missionary, especially to the Southern states. Strongly supported by women's groups and by the denomination's newly organized youth, Shinn traveled extensively, establishing churches wherever possible. Lacking trained ministers to staff these new groups or denominational structures to service them, Shinn trained cadres of lay people to provide the leadership his fledgling congregations needed. In this activity, Shinn anticipated the fellowship movement by decades.

As the century came to a close, Universalists, like most Americans, were pondering the future and seeking to understand what the times would demand of them. Like most of their contemporaries, Universalists felt that they stood on the brink of a momentous moment in human history. The new century was to be the "Christian century," the occasion when the full implications of Christian moral and ethical thought would be made manifest in human relationships and in social institutions. Universalists, like others, felt compelled to examine the social and moral implications of the faith they had professed. That compulsion would issue in the Social Gospel movement.

In 1911, the General Convention had created a Commission on Social Service, chaired by Frank Oliver Hall. Clarence R. Skinner (1881-1949), the secretary of that commission, was to become the dominant figure in defining Universalist response to the social imperatives of the times. Named Professor of Applied Theology at Crane Theological School in 1914, Skinner published a book entitled THE SOCIAL IMPLICATIONS OF UNIVERSALISM the following year. This work not only examined the social implications of Universalism, but did so in a way which encompassed a global view, unlimited by traditional Christian categories[71]

Continuing to work with the Commission, Skinner drafted on its behalf a declaration of social principles, which was adopted by the General Convention in 1917. The declaration called for:

> *First:* An Economic Order which shall give every human being an equal share in the common gifts of God and in addition all that he shall earn by his own labor.

Second: A Social Order in which there shall be equal rights for all, special privileges for none, the help of the strong for the weak until the weak become strong.

Third: A Moral Order in which all human law and action shall be an expression of the moral order of the universe.

Fourth: A Spiritual Order which shall build out of the growing lives of living men the growing temple of the living God.[72]

For Universalists, this stirring vision was soon set aside by the outbreak of the Great War that had engulfed Europe and now inexorably drew the United States into the maelstrom. Skinner, a pacifist in a country gearing up for war, found himself challenged by some of his colleagues and shunned by others. Supported by the academic community because of its respect for his fierce integrity and its commitment to freedom of speech, Skinner would continue to serve the movement as Dean of Crane Theological School at Tufts University until his death in 1949. The passing years have enhanced his reputation, leading some to call him the greatest Universalist of this century.

With the end of the "Great War," the Universalists returned to the incomplete agenda of the Commission on Social Service. In addition to its focus on economic justice, the denomination threw itself into the national discussion concerning the shape of the international order following the war, becoming a staunch advocate of the League of Nations as a vehicle for establishing a peaceful world order.

CREATING THE NEW UNIVERSALISM

The end of the First World War also found Universalists facing a growing institutional challenge, the dimensions of which they were slow to recognize. The war had changed everything. Thousands upon thousands of people had been uprooted, had seen service in foreign lands, had moved from rural areas to cities because of the demands of the war time economy. Many of them, despite the yearning for normalcy, would never return to their places of origin. The question posed by a popular song, "How're you gonna keep 'em down on the farm/ After they've seen Paree?" reflected more than a comical refrain.

The immediate effect on Universalists was a closing of many small rural churches, as the migration to cities left many of those institutions without a constituency. What is more, the immigrants from those rural churches often found no Universalist church waiting for them in their new communities. Nor did many of them feel the need to establish new urban churches for themselves. Over the decades, Universalists had won the theological struggle with mainline Christianity. Few of those churches now preached the partialist doctrines of hell-fire and damnation. This development served to rob Universalists of their unique theological issue, and served to make them unclear about the distinction between Universalism and the larger Christian community. And, of equal importance, the central organizational structures of the denomination were simply too weak to respond to these issues in a creative manner.

In some ways, an effective response to the other challenges would depend upon a new theological formulation. This was an issue that had been growing in strength for some time. In 1893, as part of the Chicago World's Fair, the Universalists had participated in the World Parliament of Religions. This unique gathering of religious communities from all over the world brought to Americans a fresh understanding of the vast variety of religious alternatives that existed. It was in connection with the World Parliament that many Americans first encountered eastern religions and particularly the mysticism of the east, finding there a vision that was both exotic and yet strangely familiar. Among Universalists the effects of this encounter was to strengthen the sense of being a church with a special mission, a mission which might be broader than Christianity, a mission to include all of humanity within the seamless circle of love and concern.

An immediate consequence of the Universalist experience in the World Parliament had been the establishment of the American Congress of Liberal Religious Societies—an effort to bring together into co-operation liberal elements within various religious communities. Included in the Congress, which received its greatest support in the Chicago area, were Unitarian, Universalist, Jewish, Quaker and Ethical Culture groups. The secretary and missionary of the group was A.N. Alcott, minister of the Universalist Church in Elgin, Illinois.

Conservatives immediately saw in the Congress a threat to the unity of the Universalist movement and particularly to its identification with its Christian roots. Alcott's fellowship was revoked on the grounds that he was serving a non-Universalist religious community. When Alcott appealed the revocation, his action was ignored. Those who supported the Congress and Alcott began talking about the need for a "new Universalism," a broader sense of the mission for Universalism in a world of increasing complexity and interaction. Thus, the stage was set for the debate which would occur in the next century as Universalists sought to define their mission and their relationship to the Christian tradition out of which they had emerged.

Circumstances seemed to conspire to force Universalists to confront the question of who they were, what the content of their gospel might be and how they related to the larger Christian community. In 1925 the Unitarians and the Congregationalists each proposed merger discussions with the Universalists. After studying the two proposals, a Universalist commission recommended "closer co-operation" with the Congregationalists, a result which left the Unitarians feeling rejected. In point of fact, however, the Universalists had no interest in merging with the Congregationalists, who ultimately sought out other partners for merger. The dynamics of this decision undoubtedly involved a concern on the part of Universalists that the Congregationalists would absorb the Universalists, and an equal concern that the Unitarians were not sufficiently rooted in the Christian traditions so dear to conservative Universalists.

Again, in 1931, the question of merger with the Unitarians was raised, and a joint merger commission was appointed. Again, Universalists were not prepared to give up their identity, but the two denominations did establish the Free Church Fellowship in 1933. The hope was that this fellowship would provide a structure through which liberal churches of many different stripes could unite their efforts and co-ordinate their programs. In the end, the Fellowship failed to gain any significant support outside of the Unitarian and the Universalist communities.

In 1933, the appearance of the Humanist Manifesto challenged all traditional religious assumptions. Of the signers of the manifesto, only Clinton Lee Scott was a Universalist minister, though Charles Francis Potter and J. A. C. Fagginer Auer held joint fellowship with the Unitarians and the Universalists. Most Universalists were not supportive of the Manifesto, with its call of a this-worldly, reason-based, non-theistic, non-supernatural religion. However, the appearance of this challenging document demonstrated anew the need for Universalists to restate their message to a changed and changing world.

In 1935, the General Convention, meeting in Washington, D. C., adopted, with little debate or controversy, a new "Bond of Fellowship and Statement of Faith:"

> The bond of fellowship in this church shall be a common purpose to do the will of God as Jesus revealed it and to co-operate in establishing the Kingdom for which he lived and died.
>
> To that end we avow our faith in:
> God as Eternal and All-conquering Love,
> The spiritual leadership of Jesus,
> The supreme worth of every human personality,
> The authority of truth, known or to be known,

And in the power of men of good will and sacrificial spirit
to overcome all evil and progressively to establish the Kingdom of God.[73]

In many ways, this statement of the essence of Universalism is a
remarkable departure from previous statements. It reflects a new
Christology—Jesus is a leader, a spiritual model but his relation to
God is left unspecified. The statement reflects a changed eschatology.
Gone is the concern about life after death, and who will be admitted
and on what terms. Instead, the Kingdom of God is the gradual result of human effort. In this respect the statement affirms the commitment to social justice which was the lasting legacy of Benjamin
Rush and Clarence Skinner. The affirmation nowhere mentions the
Bible. And, in the course of adopting this statement, the historic liberty clause was also affirmed. By 1935, if Universalism had not departed from Christianity, it had opened the door to a much broader
understanding of its mission.

The man who would walk through that door was Robert
Cummins. Chosen as General Superintendent in 1938, Cummins set
about to revitalize a demoralized movement suffering from decades
of decline. He proposed a four-point program for renewal, and set
about to restructure the denominational operation. At his suggestion, the General Convention of Universalists became the Universalist Church of America in 1942, and its delegate body came to be
known as the General Assembly. In 1943, addressing the Assembly,
Cummins offered this remarkable assessment:

Universalism cannot be limited either to Protestantism
or to Christianity, not without denying its very name. Ours
is a world fellowship, not just a Christian sect. For so long as
Universalism is universalism and not partialism, the fellowship bearing its name must succeed in making it unmistak-
ably clear that *all* are welcome: theist and humanist, unitarian and trinitarian, colored and color-less. A circumscribed
Universalism is unthinkable.[74]

Cummins was not speaking for all Universalists. Many powerful ministers were deeply committed to their Christian heritage. However, he did serve to encourage younger ministers who were restive within the constraints of that tradition. What is more, his message was given added impetus by the judgment of the larger Christian community. In 1942 and again in 1944, the Universalist Church of America sought admission to the Federal Council of Churches. On both occasions the Universalists were rejected on theological grounds—in the judgement of the Council, Universalists were insufficiently Christian in that they did not condition membership upon an affirmation of Jesus Christ as Lord and Savior. The effect of these repeated rejections was to force Universalists to reevaluate their relation to Christianity.

Unwilling or unable to meet the expectations of the larger Christian world, many Universalist leaders set about to rethink the nature of the movement they served and the peculiar gospel it offered. Angus Maclean of St. Lawrence Theological School would insist: "After being turned down twice as not being good Christians, we decided we should look somewhere else."[75] Tracey Pullman, minister of the Universalist Church in Detroit, would call for a new religion that would be greater than Christianity. Brainard Gibbons, later to serve as President and then General Superintendent of the Universalist Church of America, would insist that Christianity and the larger Universalism are irreconcilable.

From 1946 through 1954 a group of younger ministers organized themselves into a group called The Humiliati. Critics suggested that there was nothing humble about these recent graduates from Crane Theological School who set about to renew the denomination by encouraging a "universalized Universalism." Out of their discussions and concern emerged a new symbol for Universalism—a cross off-center in a circle, intended to demonstrate that while Universalism had emerged from the Christian tradition, Christianity was no longer central to the Universalist gospel. Those who took offense at this graphic representation of the new Universalism would have another cause for alarm when one of the group, David Cole, refused to be ordained to the Christian ministry as had been customary, and insisted instead on being ordained to the Universalist ministry.

In 1949, the New Universalism was incarnated in institutionalized form, when the Massachusetts State Convention established a new congregation in Boston—Charles Street Meeting House—and hired Rev. Kenneth L. Patton to be the minister for the new congregation. Patton was charged with breaking new ground and offering a clear alternative to the tradition-bound Unitarian churches in the city. Patton went to work with vigor and enthusiasm. He created a church in the round, decorated with symbols and art from the world's great religion, and as a focal point, a mural of the great nebula in Andromeda. Instead of an altar, Patton installed a shelf of books.

A prolific writer, Patton set about to refashion the liturgy of liberal churches. He wrote and published poems, readings, hymns—all reflective of a naturalistic mysticism that celebrated the human experience in its natural setting. He sang of salvation in this world; he called for justice in this world; he rejoiced in the rhythm of the seasons and he celebrated life and death. Meeting House Press, established by Patton, made the work and the experience of the experimental congregation available to the larger movement. It must be admitted that he had little patience with more conservative and traditional forms, and his lack of tact won him few friends among those who disagreed with him.

For a while, Charles Street Meeting House became the focus of the struggle between the conservative and the liberal wings of the Universalist Denomination. Although Patton held full fellowship as a Universalist minister, and despite the fact that the Massachusetts State Convention had founded and funded the Meeting House, the new congregation was refused fellowship for three years as a consequence of the antagonism of conservative Universalists. Finally, however, at a meeting of the Convention in Worcester in 1952, the Charles Street Meeting House was received into fellowship with the Universalist State Convention.

While the hope of establishing a self-supporting church in Boston was never fully realized,[76] the work Kenneth Patton did at Charles Street Meeting House was of the greatest significance for the future of liberal religion. His liturgical vision shaped the thinking and the worshiping of Unitarians and Universalists alike, providing them a common language and experiences that prepared the road to merger. Without a doubt, Kenneth Patton was one of the most important influences upon Unitarian and Universalist thought in the twentieth century.

The question of merger with the Unitarians emerged again in 1949 when a Committee on Union with the Unitarians reported to the General Assembly. In response to that report, the delegates unanimously approved a resolution calling for federal union, and referring the matter to a poll of the churches. Of the 304 certified Universalist churches participating in the poll, 220 voted approval of the proposal. The result of this effort was the "Council of Liberal Churches"—an over-arching structure which combined the publication, publicity and religious education efforts of both denominations.

As had been the case with the Free Church Fellowship twenty years before, supporters of this halfway measure hoped that other liberal religious bodies would find it advantageous to join the Council of Liberal Churches. None did, and in the end, the addition of this superstructure to the existing denominational bodies proved too cumbersome and expensive to maintain. Therefore, it was not a surprise when in 1955 a committee recommended that the General Assembly appoint members to a joint merger commission to study the possibility of some kind of organic union between the American Unitarian Association and the Universalist Church of America.

With the approval of both denominations, a twelve-member commission, drawn from both traditions, went to work. By 1958 the commission had prepared and transmitted to the churches detailed plans for the consolidation of the two bodies. Churches carefully studied the proposals in preparation for a joint meeting of the two denominations in Syracuse, NY, in the fall of 1959.

The purpose of the Syracuse meeting was to hammer out a proposal that both denominations could recommend to the churches for a plebiscite to be conducted during that church year. The Unitarian meetings were held in a local hotel; the Universalists meet at Betts Memorial Church. A telephone line connected the two deliberating bodies as they proceeded through the proposal step by step, each carefully considering any changes or amendments offered by either body.

Immediately it became clear that there would be a struggle over how to define the relationship of the new movement to the Christian tradition out of which they had emerged. After several votes, a statement of principles was adopted which did not mention Jesus, and which referred not to our Judeo Christian heritage, as originally proposed, but to the Judeo-Christian heritage. In the end, the two bodies each voted overwhelmingly to approve a single merger proposal and to send it to the churches for ratification.

The next two months saw strong efforts on both sides to sway the votes of the churches. Ellsworth Reamon of Syracuse and Cornelius Greenway of Brooklyn among others were strongly opposed to the notion of merger with the Unitarians. Among the more conservative Universalists, these men saw the merger as one more threat to their Christian faith and rallying around the cry "Cooperation but not consolidation," they mounted a spirited defense of their position. Opponents of the merger from the Unitarian camp were fearful lest the consolidation with the Universalists exert a braking effect upon the renewal and renaissance Unitarianism had been experiencing in the years after the Second World War. Unitarian Humanists were fearful of the theological conservatism of Universalists. Universalists were fearful of being contaminated by Unitarian intellectualism and even more fearful of being swallowed up by the larger body.

In truth, however, it was difficult for most to see how the merger could be avoided. Many of the largest, most influential urban churches were already merged. The two national youth groups, impatient with the overly deliberate pace of their elders, had merged in 1953 to create the Liberal Religious Youth. The churches of both denominations were using the same hymnals, the same religious education materials, and were drawing ministers from the same schools. As for theological differences, it was generally conceded that there were more differences within each communion than there was between them. And many in both groups were convinced that the merger of the two denominations would strengthen the voice of liberal religion, expand its influence and enhance its prospects. In the end, when the votes of the churches had been counted, 79% of the Universalist congregations voted for the proposal and 91% of the Unitarian congregations supported it.

There was one more formal step to take. Separate but concurrent meetings of the two denominations were called for Boston in May of 1960. There, 365 of the 430 Universalist delegates voted formally to approve the merger; while 725 of 868 Unitarian delegates gave their assent. The merger of the American Unitarian Association and the Universalist Church of America had been accomplished, and the new body, the Unitarian Universalist Association came into being in May of 1961, almost a hundred years after the first serious proposal for merger had been made.

In conjunction with the 1961 meeting, eleven churches and fellowships in Canada met to organize the Canadian Unitarian Council, a body affiliated with the Unitarian Universalist Association, but designed specifically to serve the special needs and interests of Canadian congregations. Although Universalists had been in Canada since 1804, nearly half a century before the founding of the Montreal Unitarian Church, and although at one time Universalists had greatly outnumbered Unitarians in that country, by 1961 only three small Universalist congregations remained. Those organizing the new council felt no need to include the Universalist name and thus risk public confusion about the nature of the new national body.[77]

The formal ceremonies in Boston in May 1961 brought an end to the independent existence of the oldest American-born religious denomination (excluding the religions of pre-European Americans) on this continent. The importance of the Universalist experience, as it moved from a "Calvinism stood on its head" to a vision which could not be contained within the Christian consensus, has yet to be fully explored. Nonetheless, the non-Unitarian Universalist historian, Whitney Cross suggested the scope and depth of that significance when he wrote that the impact of Universalists "on reform movements and upon the growth of modern religious attitudes might prove to be greater than that of either the Unitarians or the freethinkers. And their...warfare upon the forces fettering the American mind might be demonstrated to have equaled the influence of the transcendentalist philosophers"[78]

The Unitarian Universalists

It has been said that church mergers in the United States usually begin with two denominations, which merge and end in creating three or more denominations: the newly merged group, those recalcitrants from each of the previous groups who have refused to enter the merger and maintain their own separate existence, and perhaps a group more liberal or more conservative than any of the others, which discovered itself in the course of the debates leading up to the merger. This was not the case in the merger of the American Unitarian Association and the Universalist Church of America. Given the nature of congregational polity, which leaves much authority in the hands of the local body, and the commitment to democratic, rather than consensual process, the assumption was that the majority would rule, so long as the rights of the minority had been respected.

The process developed by the merger commission encouraged broad participation, allowed for wide expression of opinion, solicited alternative viewpoints, making certain that minority opinions would be respected. At the conclusion of the process all congregations in both denominations were assumed to be part of the new Association unless they took specific action to disassociate from the larger body. In the end, only a handful of mostly small, rural congregations chose not to become part of the Unitarian Universalist Association. Even the congregations of such stalwart opponents of merger as Ellsworth Reamon (Syracuse, NY), Cornelius Greenway (Brooklyn, NY), and Seth Brooks (Washington National Memorial) remained within the fold, however uncomfortably.

This is not to suggest that all things went smoothly. The merger of the denominational bodies did not mean that the ancillary organizations were automatically merged. Over the next few years, the Unitarian Women's Alliance and the Association of Universalist Women would combine to create the Unitarian Universalist Women's Federation; the Unitarian Service Committee and the Universalist Service Committee would become the Unitarian Universalist Service Committee; the separate Churches of the Larger Fellowship, structured as churches by mail to serve isolated Unitarians and Universalists, would combine into one body. Each of these mergers would be the result of careful discussion, negotiation and deliberation.

At the level of districts and state conventions, the pattern would be even more complex. The new denominational structure followed the Unitarian pattern of regional districts which crossed state boundaries, leaving the Universalist State Conventions, which had had a legal and financial existence apart from the Universalist Church of America, in limbo. Some conventions would choose to merge into the UUA district that served the region in which they had existed.

Others, especially some with a substantial financial endowment, would choose to maintain a parallel existence and thus retain control of their funds and resources, using them to ensure that the Universalist tradition not be lost within the new movement.

Certainly, in the early years of the Unitarian Universalist Association, it seemed to many that the Universalist contributions to liberal religion in America were in danger of being forgotten. Many Universalists felt betrayed at the outset. They had believed that an unwritten agreement existed by the terms of which neither Philip Randall Giles, Superintendent of the Universalist Church of America, nor Dana McLean Greeley, President of the American Unitarian Association would seek the presidency of the Unitarian Universalist Association. They were disillusioned when Greeley announced his candidacy for that office. In the subsequent election, Greeley was opposed by William B. Rice, Unitarian minister from Wellesley Hills, MA, and chair of the Merger Commission. Greeley won the election, thus becoming the last president of the American Unitarian Association and the first president of the Unitarian Universalist Association. Many former Universalists, including Dr. Giles, would fill important posts in the Greeley administration, but a sense of betrayal would linger among some Universalists.

That sense of betrayal was compounded when the newly merged denomination decided that a movement of approximately 152,000 adults[79] simply could not support four theological schools.[80] After an analysis of the strengths and weaknesses of each school, it was determined to withdraw financial support from Crane Theological School at Tufts University and the Theological School at St. Lawrence University. Both of these institutions, Universalist in their origins, closed their doors. To no avail had the Universalists pointed out that St. Lawrence offered a clear alternative to the other schools, with its unique focus on religious education and church administration, or that Crane was the only denominational school on the East Coast. Many Universalists felt that their sensitivities had been ignored in the name of institutional streamlining. Nor did it help matters much to point out the Universalist connections of the two remaining schools: that Thomas Starr King for whom the California school was named had been both a Unitarian and a Universalist or that the Lombard College which was part of Meadville's name and tradition had been a Universalist school.

It must be admitted also, that the inescapable tendency of people, within the movement and without, to shorten the name of the denomination from Unitarian Universalist to Unitarian added to the sense that the Unitarians had swallowed the Universalists. For years, Universalists would bristle at the omission, and for years General Assembly speakers would be reminded that the name of the movement was Unitarian Universalist.

Despite these frictions, the work of creating a new religious institution out of the dual heritage of the past went on apace. In the words of the Commission on Appraisal, "many of us were astonished that so little change took place."[81] Dana Greeley provided for many a bridge between the familiar past and the unfamiliar future, and proved to be a leader of deep, if not always well founded, optimism. Greeley confidently predicted that the growth and vitality that had characterized Unitarianism in the decade of the 1950s would be enhanced by the merger. He dreamed of a million Unitarian Universalists by the end of the century, and he invested the energies and resources of the Association in "pump-priming" projects intended to bring that dream to reality.

Nor was Dana Greeley only concerned with the internal health of the Unitarian Universalist Association. He saw Unitarian Universalism as a vital force with a mission to the larger world. As that world faced growing crises, Greeley called upon Unitarian Universalists to respond. He offered strong support to the Civil Rights movement, urging his co-religionists to affirm the moral imperatives of the drive to end segregation in the United States. Uncounted numbers of Unitarian Universalists, lay and cleric alike, answered that call, participating in marches and demonstrations, organizing fair-housing committees, lobbying congress and the White House in an effort to translate the denomination's historic commitment to justice and equity into effective action. Various congregations undertook to support urban ministries, aimed at organizing the poor, largely African American residents of the nation's inner cities. Under Greeley's leadership, the Association created a Commission on Religion and Race to spearhead work on this major priority.

It was not surprising that when Martin Luther King, Jr. issued his call to the clergy to join him in his voter registration drive in Selma, Alabama, a number of Unitarian Universalist clergy responded. Among them, was James Reeb. Having gone out to dinner one evening while in Selma, Reeb and several of his colleagues were attacked and beaten. Reeb died as a result of that attack. In response, when King announced plans to resume his interrupted march from Selma to Montgomery, the Unitarian Universalist Association urged as many as could to join in that effort. Thousands of Unitarian Universalists, including Dana Greeley, participated in various phases of that march. Following the triumphant march into the state capital, the Unitarian Universalists suffered another martyrdom when Viola Liuzzo, a member of the Detroit church, was shot and killed as she was driving back to Selma.

With this as a background, Unitarian Universalists were unprepared for the emergence within their own ranks of a demand for black power. Committed to desegregation and the creation of a racially integrated society, they had focussed little attention upon the fact that segregation was only one manifestation of racism and that the end of segregation would not signal the end of racism. They had forgotten the warning of the Universalists, who in 1853 noted that slavery was only the beginning of the problem, that ultimately "we must conquer our miserable prejudices." Over a century earlier Universalists had understood that racism was not just a Black problem; it was primarily a White problem which would demand significant changes in the dominant community. Wrapped up in the political struggles of the 1960's, Unitarian Universalists were so busy trying to change "them" they had had little time to examine the racist assumptions built into their own predominantly white, upper-middle class institution.

In 1967, responding to riots in American cities, the Unitarian Universalist Association, working through the Commission on Religion and Race and the Department of Social Responsibility, convened a conference at the Biltmore Hotel in New York City to understand the causes of urban unrest and to frame a response to "The Black Rebellion." African American participants in that conference insisted that the problem was not "the black rebellion" but the persistent insensitivity of middle-class white institutions to the need to share power with the African American community. These delegates sought and obtained an opportunity to meet apart from the White delegates. Out of the Biltmore conference came a demand for a program of action which would be funded by the Unitarian Universalist Association, but which would be largely in the hands of and directed by black Unitarian Universalists.[82]

The Black Unitarian Universalist Caucus, which emerged from the Biltmore Conference, proposed that the Commission on Religion and Race be replaced by a Black Affairs Council, nominated by the Black Caucus, and predominantly African American in its composition. The Black Affairs Council would develop and fund programs for empowerment, using funds provided by the UUA. The Caucus envisioned a fund of one million dollars, to be paid out over a four-year period.

This was not the outcome the Board of the UUA had had in mind when the Biltmore conference had been conceived. The response of the Board reflected the confusion and surprise of much of the denomination. The Unitarian Universalists, after all, had been on the side of racial justice without equivocation. They had risked much and some of them had bled and died. Moreover, they were committed to an integrated model of race relations. How could they acquiesce in a structure that appeared to be segregated at its core? More than this, Unitarian Universalists were committed to the democratic process. They did not respond well to demands or to veiled threats. The Board proposed to restructure the Commission on Religion and Race and to alter its make-up, but was unwilling to accede to the demands for a Black Affairs Council.

This set the stage for the meeting of the General Assembly in Cleveland in 1968. By the time the assembly convened, divisions within the denomination had solidified. A group of supporters of the Black Caucus' proposals had organized under the name FULLBAC, determined to achieve full support and funding of the Black Affairs Council. A second group, centered in the Community Church of New York, and under the leadership of its minister, Donald Harrington, and one of its laymen, Cornelius McDougald, an African American and former chair of the Commission on Religion and Race, organized BAWA—Black And White Alternative— committed to an integrationist program. Before the Assembly convened, both groups had campaigned for their respective positions throughout the denomination.

At the Cleveland Assembly, the issue came to a head. A proposal to fund both BAC and BAWA was defeated, an indication that the delegates understood that the issue was not only a matter of funding a program to confront the consequences of racism, but it was also a matter of who would provide leadership and direction of that program. After intense and sometimes bitter debate, the Assembly voted by more than 70% to endorse the Black Affairs Council and instructed the Board of Trustees of the Unitarian Universalist Association to fund the Council at the rate of $250,000 a year for four years.

The Board of the Unitarian Universalist Association, meeting a month later, was troubled by the fact that the structure of the Black Caucus and the Black Affairs Council seemed to violate the constitution of the UUA, which required that all affiliates refrain from the practice of segregation based on race or color. Although the Board eventually found a way around this difficulty and granted affiliate status to the Black Affairs Council, it remained uncomfortable with the challenge BAC presented. On the other hand, the Board had no difficulty granting affiliate status to BAWA, now renamed Black And White Action, a decision which many saw as defiance and repudiation of the position affirmed by the General Assembly.

When the General Assembly convened in Boston in 1969, it was clear that the debate over the Black Affairs Council was not over. The Board had scheduled a vote on a proposal to fund BAC and BAWA. The fact that the vote on this proposal was scheduled for late in the assembly led many to believe the power structure was hoping that a significant number of BAC supporters would have gone home before the vote was taken. The Black Affairs Council and its supporters regarded this proposal and its placement on the agenda as one more attempt to challenge the decision of the Cleveland Assembly to place control of the Association's anti-racism efforts in the hands of its African American members. The Black Affairs Council made it clear to the Assembly that if Black And White Action was funded by the UUA, the Council would withdraw. In a series of procedural efforts to bring the issue forward on the agenda, BAC and its supporters were defeated.

As a consequence, members of the Black Affairs Council quietly left the assembly. Jack Mendelsohn, minister of the Arlington Street Church in Boston, when recognized by the Chair, called the attention of delegates to the departure of the African Americans and declared his unwillingness to remain in the meeting. He announced that he was leaving the Assembly and would be going to the Arlington Street Church, and invited any who shared his discomfort to join him there. After a brief pause, delegates, one by one, stood up from their seats and began to follow Mendelsohn out of the meeting, until approximately 400 delegates had walked out of the Assembly.

It is hard to know who was more stunned by this unanticipated event, the delegates who remained in the meeting, or the delegates at Arlington Street Church, who referred to themselves as "the moral caucus." It is clear that both groups recognized that a critical moment had arrived in the history of the Unitarian Universalist Association. The main body sent a delegate to Arlington Street Church to invite the return of the dissidents. The moral caucus, while speaking eloquently of the issue which had moved them to leave, had no program or plan of action or organizational structure. After a time of negotiation, the caucus returned to the assembly. The assembly abided by its agenda, but in the end it declined to fund BAWA, while affirming its financial commitment to the Black Affairs Council. The pain and bitterness occasioned by what would be know in the mythology of the movement as "the walkout" would remain to influence the subsequent development of the Association, as it struggled with an ever more complex world.

Before the year was over, the UUA Board—struggling with a growing financial problem occasioned by the commitment of the General Assembly to fund the Black Affairs Council and the Board's own unwillingness to trim other costs to meet the impact of that decision—announced that it would reduce funding of the Council to $200,000 per year, thus taking five years instead of four to meet its commitment. In light of the Board's proposal, only a few months earlier, to fund Black and White Action at the rate of $50,000, this seemed one more refusal to honor the action of the General Assembly. In the end, the Black Affairs Council disaffiliated from the UUA and announced a program to raise money from Unitarian Universalist sources independently. This action brought an end to the Association's bold but controversial efforts at Black empowerment, and in many ways signaled the Association's withdrawal from vital involvement in the more radical aspects of the Civil Rights struggle.

At the Boston Assembly in 1969, Dana Greeley completed his

second term as President of the UUA and was succeeded by Rev. Robert Nelson West[83]. West's term began with a jolting recognition of the seriousness of the Association's financial situation. Debts were coming due without any plan in place to pay them. West instituted a series of cost cutting programs, which included reductions of staff at the Boston headquarters and the consolidation of the districts, most of which had previously had their own full-time executives, into a series of large inter-districts with one executive shared among several districts. The activities of the various departments at the national headquarters were cut back. The national periodical was transformed from a magazine format into a newsprint publication.

For a while it looked as if these draconian measures would prove insufficient and that perhaps the publishing arm of the movement, the Beacon Press—a widely respected, but not always profitable enterprise—would be sold. (Some Unitarian Universalists were heard to mutter that it would be better to sell the UUA and keep the Beacon Press.) In the end, the press was saved and eventually, under dedicated leadership began to show modest profits.

Like many other institutions, the Unitarian Universalist Association was caught up in the tides that were sweeping the continent and the world in the early 1970's. Dana Greeley had been an early opponent of the Vietnam War and as that conflict became a focal point of national unrest, the leadership of the Association, many of the ministers and many members of local congregations identified strongly with the growing opposition to the war. In 1972, Beacon Press published the PENTAGON PAPERS, a secret Pentagon study of the involvement of the United States in the war in Southeast Asia. Immediately, the Association found itself in a fierce confrontation with the federal government, which sought access to the Association's financial records, in an effort to determine who was identified as a supporter of the UUA. The Unitarian Universalist Association resisted this intrusion, organized a National Conference on American Freedom, and by 1974, the Justice Department had indicated that it would drop its efforts to obtain the Association's bank records.

Many Unitarian Universalists were proud of the Association and its record of outspoken opposition to the war. However, it should not be assumed that there was unanimity about the war among Unitarian Universalists. Many long-standing members vigorously objected to the position the Association had assumed, and expressed that objection by withdrawing their financial support, and in some cases, resigning their memberships. Nor was this the only point of conflict. Like many institutions, the Unitarian Universalist Association and its member congregations were shaken by the rapid changes in lifestyles, the deepening distrust of institutions, the gap between generations, the new attitudes toward sexuality which were part of the changes which swept the world in the late sixties and seventies. Times of sweeping change are difficult for religious institutions, since religions, even the most liberal, are conservative at heart, eager to find and hold on to valued patterns. Unitarian Universalism was no exception.

Reporting to the General Assembly in 1975, the UUA Commission on Appraisal noted that despite the optimism about growth which had constituted the common wisdom in the years immediately following merger, in fact, those dozen or so years had seen the adult membership of the Association drop from 152,000 to 150,000 and enrollment in church schools fall from 78,000 to 49,000.[84] While this pattern was consistent with the experience of many main-line churches during those years, it was especially alarming to an institution that had gambled its modest resources on the possibility of growth and now had only very slender reserves on which to fall back.

The Unitarian Universalists were a discouraged movement as Dr. West's term of office came to an end in 1977. There was no clear successor in view. However, the movement still possessed sufficient vitality to draw a field of three contestants for the office. After a vigorous campaign, conducted all across the continent, Dr. Paul Carnes from Buffalo, New York, emerged as the victor and became the third President of the Unitarian Universalist Association.

Dr. Carnes died after serving only two years of his term as President. However, those two years were pivotal for the Association in several ways. Carnes was a more visible president that Dr. West had been, and worked to restore morale to the movement, a process that his successor, Dr. Eugene Pickett would build upon. In addition, the Carnes administration found itself confronting an emergent movement within the association concerned with the rights of women and especially with the manifestation of sexism within the movement itself.

In 1977, the General Assembly, meeting in Ithaca, had adopted a resolution on Women and Religion, calling upon members of the Unitarian Universalist Association to examine "their own religious beliefs and the extent to which these beliefs influence sex-role stereotypes" both within families and within the religious movement itself. The resolution called upon Unitarian Universalists to "avoid sexist assumptions and language in the future." It further requested an annual report from the President of the Association on progress in implementing the resolution.[85]

In the outside world, Unitarian Universalists would seek to implement the spirit of this resolution with strong support for freedom of choice in reproductive matters. In the years before the Roe v. Wade decision that legalized abortion, a number of Unitarian Universalist clergy participated in a network that counseled women with "difficult pregnancies" and helped them find safe abortions. Similarly, the proposed Equal Rights Amendment to the federal Constitution received strong denominational support, as did the growing demand for equal pay for equal work. Unlike resolutions largely aimed at the outside world, however, this resolution resulted in sweeping changes within the Unitarian Universalist Association. From it would flow a sexism audit, a determined effort to place competent women in positions of responsibility, and a significant increase in the number of women entering the ministry and securing major pulpits. (By the end of the century, women would outnumber men in the Unitarian Universalist ministry.) Women mounted major but unsuccessful challenges to the tradition of male leadership in the office of the Presidency when Sandra Caron challenged William Shulz in 1985 and Rev. Carolyn Owen-Towle entered the contest against John Buehrens in 1993.

Perhaps the most immediate and visible result of the Women and Religion Resolution would prove to be the development of a new statement of Principles and Purposes for the Association. Taking the challenge of the resolution seriously, delegates to the General Assembly began to insist upon more inclusive language than had been customary at the time the original statement of Principles had been adopted in 1961. At the General Assembly in Philadelphia in 1981, the Women's Federation proposed major changes in the language of those principles. After an exhaustive process in which congregations across the continent were engaged in shaping and refining new language, a consensus emerged and was given preliminary approval by the General Assembly, meeting in Columbus, Ohio in 1984. The following year, the Assembly met in Atlanta, Georgia and gave final approval.

Received with great enthusiasm, the new statement soon began to appear, in one form or another, in liturgical settings, and framed on walls of meeting rooms. In that statement, Unitarian Universalists defined the covenant between them in this way:

> *We, the member congregations of the Unitarian Universalist Association, covenant to affirm and promote*
>
> *The inherent worth and dignity of every person;*
>
> *Justice, equity and compassion in human relations;*
>
> *Acceptance of one another and encouragement to spiritual growth in our congregations;*
>
> *A free and responsible search for truth and meaning;*

The right of conscience and the use of the democratic process within our congregations and in society at large;

The goal of world community with peace, liberty and justice for all;

Respect for the interdependent web of all existence of which we are a part.

The living tradition which we share draws from many sources:

Direct experience of that transcending mystery and wonder, affirmed in all cultures, which moves us to renewal of the spirit and an openness to the forces which create and uphold life;

Words and deeds of prophetic women and men which challenge us to confront powers and structures of evil with justice, compassion and the transforming power of love;

Wisdom from the world's religions which inspires us in our ethical and spiritual life;

Jewish and Christian teachings which call us to respond to God's love by loving our neighbors as ourselves;

Humanist teachings which counsel us to heed the guidance of reason and the results of science and warn us against idolatries of the mind and spirit.

Grateful for the religious pluralism which enriches and ennobles our faith, we are inspired to deepen our understanding and expand our vision. As free congregations we enter into this covenant, promising to one another our mutual trust and support[86]

In many ways, this statement managed to catch the spirit of Unitarian Universalism as it approached the end of the century. Under the leadership of Dr. Pickett, the movement began, slowly, to reverse its decline. That momentum continued into and through the two terms of William Schulz and on into the terms of his successor, John Buehrens. Indeed, as Unitarian Universalists were closing out the century, they were exhibiting a new vitality and strength. New congregations were being established, new buildings were being built, long-established congregations were growing in numbers and activities. Once more Unitarian Universalists laid claim to being one of the fastest growing religious movements on the continent.

In addition, Unitarian Universalists were seeking significant ways to carry their message to the larger community, and make it effective in the larger world. In response to policies of the Romanian government which appeared to threaten the existence of many Unitarian churches in Transylvania, a strong partner-church program was established. This initiative resulted in a steady flow of resources into Transylvania and frequent pilgrimages from North America to that ancient homeland of the faith. In 1995, the Transylvanian Unitarians, with the aid of American, British and Swiss friends, dedicated a new church building at Barot—the first new Unitarian Church building in Transylvania in fifty years, perhaps the first new building in the twentieth century—and two other buildings were under construction.

The social concerns of the movement were not limited to Eastern Europe. The Unitarian Universalist Service Committee sponsored a program in support of children in North America. Local congregations found ways to express their faith in aid to the homeless, in support of centers for reproductive freedom, and in a variety of ways. Many congregations sought ways by which they might actively welcome the gay and lesbian community, encouraging ministers to perform services of "Union" for people seeking to celebrate their commitment to partners of the same sex, and actively affirming the civil rights of all people regardless of sexual orientation.

There was nothing placid or complacent about Unitarian Universalism as it confronted the twenty-first century. As it had so often in its history, the movement burst the banks of conventional religious thought. An unexpected consequence of the feminist thrust was a sweeping reconsideration of fundamental spiritual categories. A significant number of Unitarian Universalists, rejecting Jewish and Christian assumptions, but unwilling to surrender a spiritual approach to life and unable to find the spiritual nourishment they were seeking in humanism, openly embraced a neo-pagan search for truth and meaning. Goddess worshippers and advocates of "the old religion" made their voices heard, even forcing a place for their perspective in a new hymnal, "Singing the Living Tradition", published in 1993.

Others, in a related move, began to advocate for spirituality based upon the seventh principle: "respect for the interdependent web of existence." This ecology-based spirituality drew from so-called "earth-centered" traditions, as well as scientific speculations such as the "Gaia theory" which saw the earth as a living entity. In 1995, this new thrust achieved the first amendment to the statement of Principles and Purposes adopted in Atlanta in 1985, when the General Assembly, meeting in Spokane, Washington, added to the list of traditions from which Unitarian Universalism draws, "Spiritual teachings of Earth-centered traditions which celebrate the sacred circle of life and instruct us to live in harmony with the rhythms of nature."

Still others were challenging the dominance of rationalism and humanism, within the movement. Seeking to discover a deeper spirituality, they were exploring the Jewish and Christian traditions with new eyes. In some congregations and organizations, this new openness to the old traditions generated friction between constituencies that sought their religious expression in different quarters. As the century drew to a close it was not yet clear whether as a result of all this exploring and searching Unitarian Universalism would find a distinctive voice around which to coalesce, or fall into a pattern of religious enclaves with little in common and little dialogue between the various factions.

Nor was the question of religious style and language the only issue confronting the movement. Toward the end of the Schulz administration the General Assembly began some tentative steps toward picking up the issue of racism which had been dropped as a consequence of the disruptions surrounding the struggle with Black Power. In the intervening years, Unitarian Universalism had become less and less integrated, and the reality of being a white, upper middle-class movement in a world that was profoundly diverse was increasingly painful. Gradually the movement began to confront the subtle racism that was the inescapable legacy of history, present despite the best of intentions. At the same time, Unitarian Universalists were forced to face a legacy at least as old as racism—its location in the upper middle class, and the challenge that represented to a religious community which seeks a world of equity and justice.

Part of the new awareness that emerged from this confrontation was expressed in dissatisfaction with the narrowness of the sources upon which the movement drew for its intellectual and spiritual base. Increasingly there was a demand for greater diversity within the movement, embracing new worship forms, adapting the forms of other traditions, and insisting upon presenting new and different voices.

Only time will tell how this ferment will affect the Unitarian Universalist movement. Almost certainly, the Unitarian Universalism of the twenty-first century will not return to the Jewish and Christian world from which it emerged. Almost certainly, it will not settle for the scientific rationalism of mid-twentieth century humanism. How it will blend those two sources into a religious faith adequate to a multi-cultural world will almost certainly provide a fascinating next chapter of an unfinished history.

Bibliography

Arnason, Wayne B., FOLLOW THE GLEAM: A HISTO
RY OF THE LIBERAL RELIGIOUS YOUTH MOVEMENT,
Skinner House, 1980

Carpenter, Victor H., THE BLACK EMPOWERMENT CONTRO-
VERSY AND THE UNITARIAN UNIVERSALIST ASSOCIA-
TION: 1967-1970, The Minns Lectures, 1983.

Cassara, Ernest, THE ORIGINS OF NEW ENGLAND UNIVERSAL-
ISM: ANOTHER EXCHANGE, Journal of Unitarian Universalist History, Vol XXVI, 1999.

—, UNIVERSALISM IN AMERICA, A DOCUMENTARY HISTORY,
Beacon Press, 1971.

Cole, Phyllis, MARY MOODY EMERSON AND THE ORIGINS OF
TRANSCENDENTALISM, Oxford, 1998.

Commission of Appraisal, THE UNITARIAN UNIVERSALIST
MERGER, 1961-1975, REPORT OF THE COMMISSION OF AP-
PRAISAL TO THE 14TH GENERAL ASSEMBLY OF THE UNI-
TARIAN UNIVERSALIST ASSOCIATION, UUA, 1975.

Conforti, Joseph A., JONATHAN EDWARDS, RELIGIOUS TRADI-
TION AND AMERICAN CULTURE, University of North Carolina Press, 1952.

Cross, Whitney, THE BURNED-OVER DISTRICT, Cornell University Press, 1950.

Howe, Charles A., THE LARGER FAITH, Skinner House Books,
1993.

Hughes, Peter, THE ORIGINS OF NEW ENGLAND UNIVERSAL-
ISM: RELIGION WITHOUT A FOUNDER, Journal of Unitarian
Universalist History, Vol XXIV, 1997

—, EARLY NEW ENGLAND UNIVERSALISM: A FAMILY RELI-
GION, Journal of Unitarian Universalist History, Vol XXVI, 1999.

Jones, Rufus M., SPIRITUAL REFORMERS IN THE 16TH AND 17TH
CENTURIES, Beacon Press, 1914.

Lyttle, Charles, FREEDOM MOVES WEST, Beacon Press, 1952

Miller, Perry, JONATHAN EDWARDS TO EMERSON, New England Quarterly, Dec. 1940.

Miller, Russell, THE LARGER HOPE (2 vols.) Unitarian Universalist Association, 1979, 1985

Murray, John, THE LIFE OF JOHN MURRAY, Hutichinson, Orren, 1840

Parke, David, THE EPIC OF UNITARIANISM, Beacon Press, 1957

Scott, Clinton Lee, THE UNIVERSALIST CHURCH OF AMERICA, A SHORT HISTORY, The Universalist Historical Society, 1951

Takaki, Ronald, IRON CAGES, RACE AND CULATURE IN 19TH CENTURY AMERICA, Oxford, 199o.

Wilbur Earl Morse, A HISTORY OF UNITARIAIISM, SOCINIANISM AND ITS ANTECEDENTS, Harvard University Press, 1945.

—, A HISTORY OF UNITARIANISM IN TRANSYLVANIA, ENGLAND AND AMERICA, Harvard University Press, 1952

—, OUR UNITARIAN HERITAGE, Beacon Press, 1925

Williams, George Hunston, THE RADICAL REFORMATION, Westminister Press, 1962.

Wright, C. Conrad, ed., THREE PROPHETS OF RELIGIOUS LIBERALISM: CHANNING, EMERSON AND PARKER, Beacon Press, 1964.

ENDNOTES

¹In this account, I have relied heavily on the two volumes of Unitarian History by Earl Morse Wilbur. This sketch, while it seeks to be true to the story, is of necessity, highly condensed and any errors resulting from the process of selection and narration are my responsibility.

²For example, the ubiquitous burial societies.

³Italics mine

⁴ Origen insisted that even the Devil himself would find God's love irresistible and would be restored to harmony with God.

⁵A local council declared Universalism heretical in 544 c.e.

⁶The new translation of the New Testament undertaken by Erasmus had found the basic proof text for the Trinity (I John, 5:7) to be unsupported in the earliest documents. Consequently, it had been left out of the translation.

⁷Jones, Rufus M., Spiritual Reformers in the 16th and 17th Centuries, Beacon Press, 1914, pp. 96ff. (Italics mine)

⁸A district lying between ranges of the Alps near the headwaters of the Rhine and Inn. Currently in southeastern Switzerland, it was an independent republic in the sixteenth century.

⁹Wilbur, Earl Morse, A HISTORY OF UNITARIANISM, SOCINIANISM AND ITS ANTECEDENTS, Beacon Press, 1945, p.85

¹⁰Wilbur, A HISTORY OF UNITARIANISM, VOL. I, p. 271

¹¹Wilbur, A HISTORY OF UNITARIANISM, VOL. I, p. 274

¹²Ancient tradition insists that the mysterious "Spiritus" was, in fact, Adam Pastor. However, there is no way to validate that tradition and so the identity of the stranger remains unspecified.

¹³Williams, George Huntston, THE RADICAL REFORMATION, Westminster Press, pp712-13.

¹⁴Wilbur, Earl Morse, OUR UNITARIAN HERITAGE, Beacon Press, 1925, p. 215

[15]Wilbur, Earl Morse, A HISTORY OF UNITARIANISM IN TRANSYLVANIA, ENGLAND AND AMERICA, Harvard University Press, 1952, p.40

[16]Wilbur, A HISTORY OF UNITARIANISM, VOL. II, p. 72

[17]Wilbur, A HISTORY OF UNITARIANISM, VOL. II, p.103

[18]Wilbur, A HISTORY OF UNITARIANISM, VOL. II, p.208

[19]Wilbur, A HISTORY OF UNITARIANISM, VOL. II, p.209

[20]Wilbur, A HISTORY OF UNITARIANISM, VOL. II, p.210

[21]Wilbur, A HISTORY OF UNITARIANISM, VOL. II, p.241

[22]Within a generation, all Dissenting meetings in Exeter had become unorthodox and within 50 years most of Presbyterianism had moved to the liberal camp.

[23]Wilbur, A HISTORY OF UNITARIANISM, VOL. II, p.273

[24]Wilbur, A HISTORY OF UNITARIANISM, VOL. II, p.314

[25]Wilbur, A HISTORY OF UNITARIANISM, VOL. II, p.327

[26] Wilbur, Earl Morse, *Our Unitarian Heritage* (Boston, Beacon Press, 1925) 39.

[27] Montreal

[28]Arianism is that heresy which held that while Jesus was more than man, he was not equal with God; Arminianism, named for Jacob Arminius, departed from the strict predestination taught by Calvinism, and insisted that human beings, could, by their deeds and by conscious choice affect their salvation. The first of these heresies, of course, cuts the ground out from under the Doctrine of the Trinity, while the second undermines the doctrine of divine omnipotence.

[29] Other historians question the national character of this event, seeing it as largely confined to New England. See Conforti, Joseph A., JONATHAN EDWARDS, RELIGIOUS TRADITION AND AMERICAN CULTURE, U of North Carolina Press, 1995.

[30]Wilbur, A HISTORY OF UNITARIANISM, VOL. II, p.384

[31]Wilbur, A HISTORY OF UNITARIANISM, VOL. II, p.394

[32]Frequent pulpit exchanges between settled ministers was a long

established custom in Massachusetts providing congregations an opportunity hear different voices and relieving ministers of the burden of preparing new sermons. Refusal to exchange pulpits was a serious breach of collegiality.

[33]Channing, William Ellery, UNITARIAN CHRISTIANITY, in THREE PROPHETS OF RELIGIOUS LIBERALISM: CHANNING, EMERSON, PARKER, Introduction by Conrad Wright, Beacon Press, 1964, pp. 88-9

[34]Wilbur, A HISTORY OF UNITARIANISM, VOL. II, p.432

[35]Wilbur, A HISTORY OF UNITARIANISM, VOL. II, p.433

[36]The Conference continues to this day, meeting once a year in conjunction with the General Assembly of the Unitarian Universalist Association to hear and discuss a paper by a Unitarian Universalist minister.

[37] In an essay entitled, Jonathan Edwards to Emerson, (The New England Quarterly, December, 1940), Perry Miller suggests that Emerson's Transcendentalism was firmly rooted in his Puritan heritage. Other scholars have questioned the link between the Awakening and Emerson's thought. Recently, Phyllis Cole's *Mary Moody Emerson and the Origins of Transcendentalism* suggests that Emerson's eccentric Aunt may have provided that bridge.

[38]Emerson, Ralph Waldo, THE DIVINITY SCHOOL ADDRESS, in THREE PROPHETS OF RELIGIOUS LIBERALISM: CHANNING, EMERSON, PARKER, Introduction by C. Conrad Wright, Beacon Press, 1964, pp102-3

[39]Emerson, ibid. pp107-8.

[40]Wilbur, A HISTORY OF UNITARIANISM, VOL. II, pp 457-8

[41]Parker, Theodore, THE TRANSIENT AND PERMANENT IN CHRISTIANITY, in THREE PROPHETS OF RELIGIOUS LIBERALISM: CHANNING, EMERSON, PARKER, Introduction by C. Conrad Wright, Beacon Press, 1964, pp 132-3, 143

[42] Lincoln borrowed the last line of the Gettysburg address, "government of the people, by the people, and for the people" from

Parker. See Charles Lyttle, FREEDOM MOVES WEST, Boston: Beacon Press, 1952. p. 91.

[43]Parker was not the only minister to feel the hostility of conservatives. When Channing sought to hold a memorial service for Rev. Charles Follen, he was refused permission because Federal Street Church did not wish to be associated with the memory of an outspoken abolitionist. In response, Channing while retaining the title of pastor, virtually withdrew from his ministry, leaving responsibility for the church largely in the hands of his associate, Rev. Ezra Stiles Gannet.

[44]Wilbur, A HISTORY OF UNITARIANISM, VOL. II, p.462

[45]Wilbur, A HISTORY OF UNITARIANISM, VOL. II, p.463

[46]Wilbur, A HISTORY OF UNITARIANISM, VOL. II, p. 463

[47]Wilbur, A HISTORY OF UNITARIANISM, VOL. II, p.472

[48]Wilbur, A HISTORY OF UNITARIANISM, VOL. II, p.474

[49]Wilbur, A HISTORY OF UNITARIANISM, VOL. II, p. 480 n.

[50]Wilbur, A HISTORY OF UNITARIANISM, VOL. II, p. 482

[51]Wilbur, A HISTORY OF UNITARIANISM, VOL. II, p. 483

[52]Parke, David B., THE EPIC OF UNITARIANISM, Beacon Press, 1957,pp 133-34,137.

[53] The first fellowship formed was in Boulder Colorado in 1947. Within twenty years, 687 fellowships had been formed, and 45% if the active societies affiliated with the Unitarian Universalist Association were, or had begun as fellowships.

[54]For a complete history of Universalism, see Russel Miller's two volume work, THE LARGER HOPE, Boston: UUA, 1979, 1985.

[55]Murray, John, THE LIFE OF REV JOHN MURRAY, Hutchinson, Orren, 1840, p.31.

[56]The congregation survived Relly only briefly

[57] Recently a cache of Judith Murray's letters was discovered in Mississippi, where she had lived after John's death. As those documents are explored by scholars and made available to the public, we can expect new and important insights into the life and times of

this remarkable woman.

[58] In the Journal of Unitarian Universalist History (Vol. XXIV, 1997), Peter Hughes suggests that Universalism emerged independently in the Oxford, Massachusetts area between 1770 and 1785, more heavily influenced by Enlightenment thought than by Murray's Rellyan theology. In a subsequent issue of the Journal (Vol. XXVI, 1999), Ernest Cassara disputes this suggestion and Hughes offers a further defense.

[59]Miller, Russell E., THE LARGER HOPE: The First Century of the Universalist Church in America 1770-1780, Unitarian Universalist Association, 1979, p. 36

[60] For another view of Rush, see Ronald Takaki, IRON CAGES, Oxford, 1990.

[61]Concerned about the irregular nature of his first ordination, Ballou was re-ordained in Barnard, Vermont in 1803.

[62]Scott, Clinton Lee, THE UNIVERSALIST CHURCH OF AMERICA: A SHORT HISTORY, Universalist Historical Society, 1957, p 40 n

The Winchester Profession read as follows:

Article I: We believe that the Holy Scriptures of the Old and New Testament contain a revelation of the character of God, and of the duty, interest and final destination of mankind.

Article II: We believe that there is one God whose nature is Love, revealed in one Lord Jesus Christ, by one Holy Spirit of Grace, who will finally restore the whole family of mankind to holiness and happiness.

Article III: We believe that holiness and true happiness are inseparably connected and that believers ought to be careful to maintain order and practice good works; for these things are good and profitable to men.

[63]Scott, op. cit., p. 41 n: "Yet while we adopt a general profession of belief...we leave it to the several churches and societies or to smaller associations of churches if such should be formed, within the limits

of our General Association, to continue or adopt within themselves, such more articles of faith...as may appear to them best under their particular circumstances, provided they do not disagree with our general profession or plan."

[64]It has been said that if Ballou had a serious fault, it was his belief that he could write hymns.

[65] Cassara, Ernest, UNIVERSALISM IN AMERICA, A DOCUMENTARY HISTORY, Beacon Press, Boston, 1971, pp166-167

[66]Howe, Charles A., THE LARGER FAITH, Skinner House, 1993, p125.

[67]The Unitarians were part of the religious establishment (i.e. they were "anti-disestablishmentarian"). This, along with the fact that most Unitarians were Federalists, while the Universalists tended to be Jeffersonian democrats, contributed to the lack of fraternal relations between the two groups.

[68]Howe,THE LARGER FAITH, p. 68

[69]The conditions of fellowship in this convention shall be as follows:

I. The acceptance of the essential principles of the Universalist faith, to wit: The Universal Fatherhood of God; the spiritual authority and leadership of His Son, Jesus Christ; the trustworthiness of the Bible as containing a revelation from God; the certainty of just retribution for sin; the final harmony of all souls with God. The Winchester Profession is commended as containing these principles, but neither this, nor any other precise form of words is required as a condition of fellowship, provided always that the principles above stated be professed.

II. The acknowledgement of the authority of the General Convention and assent to its laws. Howe, op. cit., p. 82.

[70]Arnason, Wayne B. FOLLOW THE GLEAM: A History of the Liberal Religious Youth Movements, Skinner House, 1980, p 10.

[71]Howe, THE LARGER FAITH, p. 92.

[72]Howe, THE LARGER FAITH, p. 94.

[73]Scott, THE UNIVERSALIST CHURCH OF AMERICA, p. 40n

[74]Howe, THE LARGER FAITH, p 108.

[75]Howe, THE LARGER FAITH, p 109.

[76]After the merger, outside financial support would be withdrawn from the Meeting House, and after the departure of Kenneth Patton to a new ministry in Ridgewood, N. J., the congregation was served by Patton, who flew back to Boston for Friday eventing services, and by his associate, Alan Seaburg. Subsequently, the Meeting House was served by Randy Gibson, but after a few years the experimental congregation ceased to exist.

[77] For a full discussion of Canadian Unitarianism, see Hewett, Phillip, UNITARIANS IN CANADA, Fitzhenry and Whiteside, Toronto, 1978.

[78]Cross, Whitney, THE BURNED OVER DISTRICT, Cornell University Press, Ithica, NY, 1950, p 323.

[79]THE UNITARIAN UNIVERSALIST MERGER, 1961-1975, REPORT OF THE COMMISSION ON APPRAISAL TO THE FOURTEENTH GENERAL ASSEMBLY OF THE UNITARIAN UNIVERSALIST ASSOCIATION, 1975, p.27

[80]Meadville Theological School in Chicago, Starr King School for Ministry in Berkeley, CA, Crane Theological School at Tufts University, Medford, MA, and St. Lawrence Theological School in Canton, NY. Harvard Divinity School, though still a site for training Unitarian Universalist ministers, had become independent of the denomination.

[81]Report of the Commission on Appraisal, p. 26.

[82]For a fuller account see Carpenter, Victor H., THE BLACK EMPOWERMENT CONTROVERSY AND THE UNITARIAN UNIVERSALIST ASSOCIATION: 1967-1970, The Minns Lectures 1983.

[83]Greeley returned to the parish ministry, serving the church in Concord,MA, until his death.

[84]Report of the Commission on Appraisal, p. 27.

[85]Contrast this action with the report of Russell Miller: "A reso-

lution was offered at the General Convention (Univeralist) in 1863 acknowledging the contributions of women, especially during the Civil War. The resolution might have been adopted if it had not also urged recognition of the social, intellectual, and political rights of women and had not called for the elimination of all manifestations of belief in the inferiority of women." Miller, THE LARGER HOPE, VOL I, p.539.

[86]Directory of the Unitarian Universalist Association, 1986, p. 362.

NOTES

INDEX

B

P

Q

R

Printed in the United States
1062800003B/262-279